And That's The Gospel Truth!

What lies behind the Gospels!

By Eileen McCourt

And That's the Gospel Truth!

What lies behind the Gospels!

By Eileen McCourt

And That's the Gospel Truth! - what lies behind the Gospels! This book was first published in Great Britain in paperback during September 2016.

ISBN-13: 978-1537087917

CONTENTS

Page

ABOUT THE AUTHOR

Eileen McCourt is a retired school teacher of English and History, with a Master's degree in History from University College Dublin.

She is also a Reiki Grand Master teacher and practitioner, having qualified in Ireland, England and Spain, and has introduced many of the newer modalities of Reiki healing energy into Ireland for the first time, from Spain and England.

Eileen holds regular workshops and healing sessions in Elysium Wellness, Newry, County Down; Angel Times, Limerick; Blue Moon, Derry.

This is Eileen's seventh book.

Previous publications include:

•'***Living the Magic'***, published December in 2014

•'***This Great Awakening'***, September 2015

•'***Spirit Calling! Are You Listening?'***, January 2016

•'***Working With Spirit'***, January 2016

•'***Life's But A Game! Go With The Flow***!', March 2016

•'***Rainbows, Angels and Unicorns!'***, April 2016

All publications are available from Amazon online and are in Angel and Holistic centres around the country, as specified on website.

Eileen is currently working on her eighth book, ***'The Almost Immaculate Deception***', which exposes the scam perpetrated over the last 2,000 years by those who distorted, exploited and manipulated the life of the man known as Jesus of Nazareth, in pursuit of their own mercenary gains and lust for power.

Eileen lives in Warrenpoint, County Down, Northern Ireland.

Website: www.celestialhealing8.co.uk

e-mail: mccourteileen@yahoo.co.uk

ACKNOWLEDGEMENTS

I wish to thank my publishers, Don Hale OBE and Dr. Steve Green for all their work.

My sincere thanks also, to all my friends who encouraged me to write this book, and without whose constant support it would never have materialised!

You all know who you are!

Thank you to each and all of you who are buying my books and cd's and for your kind and generous comments!

My thanks to all those who have written reviews for me!

And of course, thank you Spirit, for the wonderful life force that runs through all of us, and for the continuous blessings and gifts that fill our lives!

Eileen McCourt

4th September 2016

AUTHOR'S NOTE

Please note, that in keeping with modern scholarly designations in dating, I have used throughout this book C.E. instead of A.D., and B.C.E. instead of B.C.

C.E. means Common Era and refers to the years from the beginning of the first century onwards to modern times.

B.C.E. means Before the Common Era, and refers to the years before the first century.

Also, for the sake of clarity, I have referred to the Gospels just simply as Matthew, Mark, Luke and John, even though these Gospels were not written by those particular named persons. These are just the names by which we know and recognise them.

Finally, there is no bibliography attached.
And that is simply because there is no need for such!

The only book you need with you is a copy of the Bible. The version used here is the Sunrise Good News Bible, published by Collins, I.S.B.N. 978-0-00-716656-5

And in fact, you do not even need this, as I have sourced all the quotations and references I have used.

Unless, of course, you want to check up on me and see that I am indeed, telling ***the Gospel truth!***

REVIEWS

" This book is definitely a 'page turner' and a fascinating read. It is a thought provoking piece of work. The author examines the Gospels from a historical perspective and focuses on the accuracy of their content. Therein lies the significance of this book as we all search for the truth behind our beliefs. Be prepared to be shocked, surprised and perhaps shaken by the historical facts that are clearly laid out for the reader.

Make up your own mind!

The Gospels appear to be pure spin and not the words of the God we know, but twisted words to suit an end that is a million miles away from the truth. This book challenges our belief in the image of a vengeful, evil, judgemental deity who takes joy in punishing us for a slight misdemeanour – based on the Gospels!

What will people think after reading the book? Some readers won't like what they read and will take offence. But I am sure that there are many who will punch the air in joy and say "I knew it!"

Will this book confuse the reader? It might, but for me, it is a refreshing view of what I am supposed to believe - according to the Church !!! The contradictions are amazing.

I enjoyed reading this book and I will be reading it again and again."

Kathleen McAlinden

Psychic

"There is no doubt that this is a thought-provoking book; within is a cauldron of delicacies which will spill into many a late night discussion, into the wee small hours!"

Clare Bowman
Spiritual Historian

The Holy Bible is the bestselling book in the history of publishing, speaking to the world's 2.3 million Christians. For 2000 years, it has impacted massively on our historical and philosophical landscape. So, how accurate and verifiable is this hugely significant document? How accurately does this portray Jesus Christ, the man and Jesus Christ, the Spirit?....and who dares to question??

In, 'And That's the Gospel Truth', Eileen McCourt, in her inimitable style, has taken the yoke and accepted this challenge. This has proven to be a huge ball of string to untangle. Untangle it she has, however, with, what some would call, unsettling conclusions. McCourt has unearthed huge historic inaccuracies, dramatically inconsistent accounts and clearly blatant fabrications. Remember, this is the document that informs the social, moral, political and spiritual lives of a significant percentage of the world's population??

McCourt has taken this 'hot potato' and dissected it in the most forensic way. She has found that much of the original manuscripts were tampered with and edited for political and social gain. Surprisingly, the identities and motives of some of the main players are hugely in doubt. It would appear that the basic facts of 'The Greatest Story Ever Told', are inconsistent and at best, sketchy.

What comes out at the end, is far from believable and ultimately questions the foundation of possibly the most significant institution in human history. So was there a 'real' Jesus Christ? If so, what was his 'real' story and more importantly, what were his 'real' teachings?

You decide.

Read on.

Another fearless, enlightening gem from Eileen McCourt.

Declan Quigley of Anam Nasca

Declan Quigley of Anam Nasca is a Shamanic Practitioner, Writer and Tutor living in Co. Down, Ireland. To Contact Declan, visit anamnasca.wordpress.com, Anam Nasca on Facebook, or drop him a line on anamnasca@gmail.com

FOREWORD

Like most other people in this country, I have sat Sunday morning after Sunday morning, bound in Spiritual fetters, submissive, obedient, believing, as the Word of God was thundered out from the pulpit, some of us listening, most of us not.

Probably the only reason most of us were there at all in the first place, was the dire threat of the punishment for not being there - a mortal sin on the soul, and if one died in that state, then an everlasting hell awaited.

And who, indeed would not attend under such circumstances?

A captive audience indeed!

One just did not question; one just believed; one just accepted.

One just accepted that what was written in the Old and the New Testaments was the inspired word of God. What was written therein was not to be questioned or criticised. Such an unwise, reckless and foolhardy course of action incurred the wrath of the Church, with the condemnation of the most unpardonable slander and heresy.

The ecclesiastical message was always to believe and stay quiet; not to protest against those to whose teachings one had been subjected since infancy. Usurpation of thought was complete, with the many long, probing, sinewy fingers of the Church extending into every aspect of life, any protest or rebellion within the ranks quickly suppressed.

The writings of the Old and the New Testaments were, we were taught, the foundation stone upon which our whole faith was built.

The Gospels, the Letters of Paul and the Acts of the Apostles spelt out the truth about Jesus and his teachings.

So what is the meaning of the title of this book?

We have all heard many times, and probably used the old appendage, "***And that's the Gospel truth!***" in an honest attempt to bolster up the truth of a particular story or statement!

Such naivety!

Such irony!

It is even more ironic when we consider that we most probably did not even know it was ironic!

In 1978, Archbishop Oscar Romero of San Salvador wrote: "*.... A gospel that doesn't unsettle, a word of God that doesn't get under anyone's skin, ... what gospel is that?*"

And again: "*To educate is to create a critical spirit and not just transfer knowledge*".

And that's the Gospel truth!

And why have I chosen such a title for this book?

The answer lies in the material included in this book.

It is time for those of us who are still asleep to waken up!

It is time for us to waken up to the truth that these writings in the Old and New Testaments abound in irreconcilable contradictions and differences, historical inaccuracies, fabrications, and a plethora of highly improbable and absolutely incredible and impossible happenings.

It is time for us to waken up and ask some serious questions about the contents of the Old and the New Testaments!

And what questions do we so urgently need to ask?

We need to ask questions about the authenticity, the validity, the trustworthiness of these writings upon which the teachings of the Catholic Church are founded.

We need to question that if these are considered to be the inspired word of God, then how come there are so many irreconcilable and blatant contradictions?

Which bits are '*inspired*' and which bits are not?

And there is only one conclusion we can possibly reach!

The dots just do not join up!

The ***figures just do not tally!***

The pieces of the jig-saw just do not fit!

Doubtless, some readers will be surprised by this book; others may well be shocked. But the shock only comes from the realisation that what has been accepted for so long to be the truth is now giving rise to so many questions.

The truth will always out, and the "*truth will make you free!*"

And so it is!

The truth about the Old and the New Testaments is there in the writings for anyone to find; anyone, that is, who is ready to face and accept the truth!

The Old and the New Testaments are not historical documents. They are theological documents. That does not mean that one needs to be a theologian or one trained in biblical studies to read them! Far from it! They can be read by anyone!

Anyone, that is, who is interested in finding the truth!

And only when we accept the truth that these writings are not the truth, only then can we begin our search to find the real truth!

To find the real Jesus!

And it was in the process of searching for the real Jesus for my next book, '***The Almost Immaculate Deception'***, in my search for the real, historical Jesus, and not the Jesus of faith or religion, that I was led to *really* read the Gospels.

And in *really* reading the Gospels, I was forced to finally accept that much of what I had believed in all along was not the truth at all!

The truth does not lie in the Gospels!

It became a game for me, and I must admit, a very entertaining game!

The contradictions are staring the reader right in the face!

The discrepancies and inaccuracies just jump out from between the pages, as if finally released from their long captivity, screaming to be identified, yearning to be recognised, wanting to be acknowledged!

The holes are there, all for the picking!

Much like finding a ripe strawberry hidden deep down in the strawberry bed, or a ripe blackberry hidden deep in the blackberry bush, "*Look! There's one! There's another! And another!*"

In no time at all, I had found enough contradictions and holes to, literally, fill a book!

And this is that book!

It is only when we line them all up together and when we *really* read them, that we find the discrepancies, contradictions and failings in the Gospels, the Acts and the Pauline Letters.

There will, no doubt, and thankfully, be readers who will agree with at least some of the suggestions, hypotheses and conclusions that I have put forward in this book.

All you need is an open mind, an unbiased judgement and above all, a sense of humour!

And of course, a copy of the Old and New Testaments!

There is definitely one thing that can be said in their favour! They make entertaining reading!

But! As far as being reliable evidence for the life of Jesus,

The dots just do not join up!

The figures just do not tally!

The jig-saw pieces just do not fit!

I invite you to come with me now, through the stages, step by step, to see how I have reached the conclusion that the writings in the Old and the New Testaments can no longer be taken as the basis for the story of the life of the man we know as Jesus.

We will not find him in there amongst those pages!

We will not find him in the stable in Bethlehem!

The bible has been described as the **'Greatest Story Ever Told!'**

That's just what it is!

A story!

A story as opposed to the **Greatest Story Never Told!** - the **Truth!**

The **Greatest Story** has yet to be told!

Finding the real Jesus, and not the Jesus portrayed to us in the writings of the New and the Old Testaments, finding the real Jesus of history, and not the Jesus of faith, not the Jesus of religion, is for another time, another day, another book.

Let us first, in this book, dispel the myths!

Then we can find the truth!

What wonderful, blessed times lie ahead!

And that's the Gospel truth!

And so be it!

Eileen McCourt

4th September 2016

CHAPTER 1:

WHAT ARE THE OLD AND THE NEW TESTAMENTS?

Christianity is a relatively young religion, less than two thousand years old. Relatively young, that is, when compared to, for example, Hinduism, Taoism, Buddhism or Judaism, all of which pre-date Christianity by thousands of years.

Christianity, in fact, grew out of Judaism.

Judaism is the parent religion; Christianity the off-spring.

Judaism and Christianity are linked in the Bible, which is the central foundation text of Christianity.

The Bible is made up of two parts, which are called the Old Testament and the New Testament.

The Old Testament is the name given to the first section of the Christian Bible, while the New Testament is the name given to the second part.

The Old Testament is based primarily on the Hebrew Bible, the Tanakh, a collection of religious writings by ancient Israelites, written centuries before the birth of Jesus.

The New Testament is the writings of the early Christian Church, all written after the death of Jesus.

As the literary archive of the ancient nation of Israel, the Hebrew

Bible is believed by most Christians and Jews to be the sacred, inspired Word of God.

The Old Testament includes the books dealing with the Law, such as Genesis, Exodus, Leviticus, Numbers, Numerology and writings of the prophets; historical books such as Joshua, Samuel, Kings, Nehemiah; poetic books such as Job, Psalms, Proverbs, Ecclesiastes, Song of Songs, Lamentations; writings of major prophets such as Isaiah, Jeremiah, Ezekiel and Daniel, and minor prophets such as Hosea, Micah, Zechariah and Malachi.

The writings of the prophets is the largest section of the Hebrew Bible and of the Old Testament. We can really say that these prophecies are history given to us in prophecy, history of the future!

The New Testament, on the other hand, can be seen as more or less the fulfillment of these prophecies of the Old Testament.

The New Testament discusses the teachings and the person of Jesus, his life, death and resurrection, as well as events in first century Christianity.

The New Testament is composed of four parts.

First, we have the four narratives of the life, teachings, death and resurrection of Jesus, as allegedly related by Matthew, Mark, Luke and John. These are known as the '*Canonical Gospels*', because they form the '*canon*' of the Christian church, the word '*Gospel*' itself meaning '*Good News*'.

Secondly, in the New Testament we have the narrative of the

Apostles' ministries in the early Church. This narrative is what is called '*The Acts of the Apostles*' and covers the post-Jesus days.

Thirdly, we have twenty one letters, often called '*Epistles*' from the Greek word '*Epistole',* written by various authors, and consisting of Christian doctrine, counsel, instruction and attempts to resolve various conflicts within the Church. Amongst these twenty one letters, there are thirteen which have the name Paul as the first word, hence claiming authorship by Paul the Apostle. It is generally now accepted by most scholars, though, that of the thirteen, only seven were actually written by Paul himself, with the other six written by others in his name.

Amongst the other letters, we also have letters from Peter and John, and from two of Jesus' brothers, James and Jude.

And yes! Jesus had brothers! And sisters too! This we shall see in our analysis of the Canonical Gospels in chapter 6!

Finally, in the New Testament we have the '*Apocalypse',* the Book of Revelation, which is a book of prophecy, containing instructions to seven local congregations of Asia Minor, but mostly containing prophecies about the end times.

These writings, all combined in the New Testament, are what we call '*Sacred Scripture',* written over the course of decades and solidified over the centuries into the Church Canon we have today. But we must remember, before there were any New Testament writings, there were the eye-witnesses to the life of Jesus himself.

So, in the New Testament, we have the four Gospels of Matthew, Mark, Luke and John, in that order, followed by Acts, and then the writings and letters of Paul, Peter, John, James and Jude.

That is the order and sequence in which they have always been presented to us, the order in which we have always been led to believe they were written.

The four Gospels come first, starting with Matthew; then Mark; then Luke and finally John. Then follows the post-Jesus narrative of Acts of the Apostles. And then come the letters and writings of Paul and the others.

However, this is not exactly the truth, which is very obvious if we look at the date of each!

The Gospels actually preceded the Epistles in oral traditions only, following the Epistles in official writing. The Gospels were therefore a distillation of oral traditions.

It is actually Paul's letters that come first, written about 50-60 C.E.

Then come the four Gospels, written over a 25 to 30 year span, from about 70-100 C.E.

This means that the writers of the Gospels already had before them the letters of Paul, and his beliefs about the teachings of Jesus. Paul never knew Jesus or never even met Jesus. Paul was the self-proclaimed apostle, arriving on the scene only after the death of Jesus. Yet Paul's writings are the earliest existing Christian writings known to historians, written twenty years after the death of Jesus.

Paul claimed that his knowledge came from a series of visions and appearances to him by Jesus after the alleged resurrection. So, according to Paul, he had personal acquaintance with, and detailed knowledge, divulged to him, and to him only, of the life of Jesus, as revealed to him personally, through visions, by the risen Christ.

So our man Paul could most certainly claim to be a man of great vision!

We know about Paul not only from his own letters, which are in most part semi- autobiographical, but also from the Acts of the Apostles, which is an account of Paul's own life, an account in which Paul himself plays the starring role.

Every good story has a hero!

And just as Jesus is the hero in the Gospels, so Paul is the hero figure in Acts.

In actual fact, it is Paul, and not Jesus, who dominates most of the New Testament!

The New Testament, as we have seen, has been presented to us differently from reality. We have been presented with the four Gospels first, and then Acts and then Paul's letters. But, as we have seen, it is Paul's letters that actually come first, according to the dates. So Paul is present in the New Testament right from the very start, and the writers of the Gospels would have had his letters before them as they wrote the Gospels, and so would have been influenced by them. So we have Paul's theories running through the Gospels as well.

And who wrote the Acts?

The Acts were written by none other than the same author who wrote the Gospel of Luke, an admirer and follower of Paul! In fact, Acts is really a continuation of the Gospel of Luke, written about 90 C.E.

The four Gospels!

Matthew, Mark, Luke and John. Their names run off our tongues like a nursery rhyme!

These Gospels were not written until forty years after the death of Jesus. The stories and details were passed down orally during that time, and it was not until forty years later that the writers began to write down all they had heard about the life of the man known as Jesus of Nazareth.

So they are a collection of stories associated with Jesus and passed down orally for forty years after his death, and it was only then that someone began to write these stories down.

The first Gospel written was actually that of Mark, written in 70 C.E.

Then came the Gospel of Matthew, written between 80 and 85 C.E.

Next came the Gospel of Luke, 85 to 90 C.E.

Next the Acts, written by Luke as a continuation of his Gospel.

Finally, John's Gospel, written between 90 and 100 C.E., towards the end of the first century C.E., by which time Jesus would have been dead for over sixty years.

This gives us a 25 to 30 year span between the four Gospels.

The names of the alleged authors are traditional names for that time and the actual authors never actually identify themselves by name. So they are all written anonymously. They are not written in the first person narrative, but rather describe the disciples in the third person narrative, which distances the authors from the action.

The first three Gospels written, Mark, Matthew and Luke are referred to as the '*Synoptics*', because of the close literary connection between them.

Mark's Gospel, the first one, written in 70 C.E. provides us with the basic narrative framework of the life of Jesus of Nazareth.

Then Matthew, ten years later, 80 to 85 C.E. uses Mark as his main source. So we have what is mostly a repeat of the original Gospel of Mark.

Luke, writing 85 to 90 A.D., follows the same pattern to some extent, but also changes some material and adds some of his own.

Finally, John, 90 to 100 or so C.E., is more theologically oriented, offering us an entirely independent version, focusing on Jesus as the Divine and exalted Son of God. A Jesus hardly recognisable from the previous three Gospels!

So if this is the order in which they actually appeared, why have we been presented with Matthew as being the first?

The obvious reason is that Matthew starts with the birth of Jesus, a natural and obvious place to start with anyone's story. Whereas, if you start with Mark, then Mark starts with the Baptism of the adult

Jesus.

So even though Mark is actually the first Evangelist, the church has always presented Matthew as being the first.

The writers of the Gospels were highly educated, highly literate and skilled, and certainly not from the lower classes of society at that time, such as poor fishermen, who would have been illiterate and uneducated. The Gospels were first written in Greek, and not in the language of Aramaic, which was the language spoken by Jesus and those around him. Aramaic is a Semitic language, related to Hebrew, Arabic and similar languages. At the time of Jesus, Aramaic was the most common language in Judea. The widespread use of Aramaic among Jews is clearly evidenced by the fact that portions of the Old Testament were written in Aramaic, and not Hebrew. Those who wrote the Gospels certainly had no difficulty in finding words to express themselves. Not being around Jesus himself, and writing later than Jesus, they could not possibly have been witnesses to what was said or done.

So, to recap, in order of date, we have, first Paul's letters, written 50-60 C.E. Then we have the Gospel of Mark, 70 C.E., then Matthew, 80-85 C.E., then Luke, 85-90 C.E., and then John, 90-100 C.E. Finally, we have the Acts. Paul himself was beheaded by the Romans in 67 C.E. during the reign of Nero, so we can see that all of the four Gospels were written after his death.

All of these writings are included in the New Testament, and the first person to list the Christian Canon of the New Testament was the Church father Athanasius, in the year 367 C.E.

In his 39th Festal Letter, in 367, Athanasius wrote: *"......I must without hesitation mention the scriptures of the New Testament; they are the following: the four Gospels according to Matthew, Mark, Luke and John, and after them the Acts of the Apostles, and the seven so-called catholic epistles of the apostles, namely, one of James, two of Peter, then three of John and after these one of Jude. In addition, there are fourteen epistles of the apostle Paul written in the following order: the first to the Romans, then two to the Corinthians and then after these the one to the Galatians, following it the one to the Ephesians, thereafter the one to the Philippians, and the one to the Colossians and two to the Thessalonians and the epistle to the Hebrews and then immediately two to Timothy, one to Titus and lastly the one to Philemon............These are the springs of salvation, in order that he who is thirsty may fully refresh himself with the words contained in them. In them alone is the doctrine of piety proclaimed. Let no one add anything to them or take away anything from them....."*

In actual fact, the letter to the Hebrews, that Athanasius includes in the letters he claims are written by Paul, has no authorship claim in it at all by anyone.

And Athanasius clearly specified "*four Gospels*".

The four Gospels of "*Matthew, Mark, Luke and John*".

And it was this Christian Canon, the Gospels of Matthew, Mark, Luke and John; the Acts of the Apostles and the letters of Paul, and, very specifically, in that particular order, which became the basis of the teachings of the Roman Catholic Church.

We will be taking a look at each of these writings in turn, not in the order in which they have been presented to us, but in the correct order and sequence, the order and sequence in which they were actually written, because it is only in looking at them in this way that we can begin to really understand what lies within them.

And in looking at them in the correct order in which they were actually written, we can reach a conclusion as to why the Church has presented them in a completely different order! The order of the four Gospels first, then the Acts, followed by the letters of Paul.

Instead of the correct order of Paul's letters first, then the Gospels and Acts following.

Why would the Church have done this? What motive lay behind their actions?

We shall see!

CHAPTER 2:

THE PROPHECIES IN THE OLD TESTAMENT

All Jewish people were familiar with and knew well the ancient prophecies in the Old Testament about how God was coming to rescue his chosen people from the oppression of the foreign invaders, the Romans, through a Messiah who would be born to them.

The society into which Jesus was born was awash with self-proclaimed Messianic preachers travelling the entire country, all claiming to be the expected Messiah, and all raising the hopes and expectations of the Jewish nation suffering under Roman oppression.

The Old Testament includes over fifty different clear prophecies of the coming of the Messiah, with over three hundred references, all indicating to the Israeli people how they would be able to recognise the Messiah when he did come.

And all the different fractious sects in Jewish Palestine, including the Pharisees, the Sadducees, the Essenes, the Zealots, seemed to have a different expectation of what exactly the Messiah would be like.

Some expected a fighter who would lead an armed insurrection and rid Israel of the hated Romans. Others expected a king who would annihilate the present world and build a new, peaceful world from among the ruins. Yet others saw him as a prophet or priest who would restore, in some way, the Jews to their previous positions of power and glory.

Jesus, throughout the Canonical Gospels, several times says that he is fulfilling a prophecy of the Old Testament. For example, in Luke's Gospel, after his Resurrection, he told his disciples: "*These are the very things I told you about while I was still with you: everything written about me in the Law of Moses, the writings of the prophets, and the Psalms had to come true............This is what was written: 'The Messiah must suffer and must rise from death three days later, and in his name the message about repentance and the forgiveness of sins must be preached to all nations, beginning in Jerusalem'.*" (Luke: 24:44-47)

Again: *"If you had really believed Moses, you would have believed me, because he wrote about me".* (John 5: 46)

So here we have clear indications, from the Gospels, that Jesus knew about the prophecies in the Old Testament.

Let us look at some of these prophecies, with which Jesus was apparently familiar!

First, the Messiah would be like Moses: "*Then Moses said: 'He will send you a prophet like me from among your own people, and you are to obey him........ He will speak in my name'.*" (Deuteronomy 18:15)

The Messiah would be of the house of David: "*The Lord says: The time is coming when I will choose as king a righteous descendant of David.'* " (Jeremiah 23: 5)

The Messiah would be born in Bethlehem: "*The Lord says: 'Bethlehem Ephrathah, you are one of the smallest towns in Judah, but out of you I will bring a ruler for Israel, whose family goes back to ancient times.'* " (Micah 5:2)

The Messiah would be hated for no reason: "*Those who hate me for no reason are more numerous than the hairs of my head; My enemies tell lies against me; they are strong and want to kill me".* (Psalms 69:4)

The Messiah will enter Jerusalem on a donkey: "*Look, your king is coming to you! He comes triumphant and victorious; but humble and riding on a donkey, on a colt, the foal of a donkey".* (Zechariah 9:9)

The Messiah would be betrayed by a friend: *"Even my best friend, the one I trusted most, the one who shared my food, has turned against me".* (Psalms 41:9)

And more specifically, he would be betrayed for 30 pieces of silver: "*So they paid me 30 pieces of silver as my wages*". (Zechariah 11:12)

The Messiah would not defend himself: "*He was treated harshly, but endured it humbly; he never said a word. Like a lamb about to be slaughtered, like a sheep about to be sheared, he never said a word". (Isaiah* 53:7)

The Messiah will be beaten and spat upon: "*I bared my back to those who beat me. I did not stop them when they insulted me....... and spat in my face".* (Isaiah 50:6)

The Messiah will be pierced: *"They will look at the one they stabbed to death*". (Zechariah 12:10)

The Messiah's hands and feet will be pierced: "*They tear at my hands and feet. All my bones can be seen*". (Psalm 22:16-17)

They will draw lots for his clothes*: "They gamble for my clothes and divide them amongst themselves*". (Psalm 22:18)

The Messiah will say: "*My God, my God, why have you abandoned me?"* (Psalms 22:1)

The Messiah will be raised from the dead*: "You protect me from the power of death.... you will not abandon me to the world of the dead".* (Psalm 16:10)

The Messiah will ascend into heaven: "*He goes up to the heights*". (Psalm 68:18)

The Messiah will perform many miracles: "*The blind will be able to see and the deaf will hear. The lame will leap and dance, and those who cannot speak will shout for joy*". (Isaiah 35:5-6)

These are just some examples of the numerous prophecies mentioned in the Old Testament writings.

We will be looking at these prophecies again, and their fulfillment, in chapter 7, but for now, suffice to say that these examples serve our purpose in showing that these prophecies were known by the Jews and by Jesus, as we shall see.

And, more importantly, as we shall also see, by the writers of the Gospels!

Are any alarm bells beginning to ring?

Are any of the dots joining up?

Are the figures starting to tally?

Are the jig-saw pieces beginning to fit?

CHAPTER 3:

THE PAULINE LETTERS IN THE NEW TESTAMENT

Of the twenty one letters included in the New Testament, fourteen are claimed by an author who appears to identify himself as Paul. Hence these are known as the Pauline Epistles, written around 59 A.D., almost thirty years after the death of Jesus, and the first of all the New Testament writings.

These Epistles, which make up the bulk of the New Testament, are letters written by the Apostle Paul to the churches he was instrumental in founding in various cities. As such, they are the first written sources we have for the early years just after the death of Jesus.

What do we learn about the life of Jesus from these letters?

Very little!

And what do we learn about the character of Paul from these letters?

A great deal!

In fact, Paul's letters are semi-autobiographical, the most important person being Paul himself, the hero of his own writings!

In the New Testament, Paul's writings have been presented as coming after the Gospels, but it is important for us to remember that in actual fact, they pre-date the Gospels.

Paul's letters were the first of the New Testament writings, written about 59 C.E., about thirty years after the death of Jesus.

So why, we have to ask, has the Church rearranged the order in which the writings in the New Testament were written, to present Paul's writings as coming after the Gospels?

What could have been the possible motive for this?

It was obviously something to do with the contents of Paul's writings!

And obviously, it was something to do with what Paul wrote, that needed to be hidden until after the Gospels were read! All the more remarkable when we consider the fact that the letters of Paul are wholly detached from any event in Jesus' life except for his Crucifixion and Resurrection and a brief reference to the Last Supper.

And obviously too of course, it was necessary to disguise the fact that the writers of the Gospels, writing after Paul, were influenced by Paul's writings!

So what then, do these letters contain?

Why did Paul put such great significance on the Death and Resurrection of Jesus, and yet fail to mention any other aspects of the life of Jesus? Why is it just all about the Death of Jesus for Paul? And about the Resurrection?

As we shall see, the Gospel that Paul created and preached differed greatly from the Gospel that Jesus and his disciples proclaimed to the Jews.

The Gospel of Jesus was known as '*The Way'*, and his followers '*Followers of The Way'.* Jesus' teachings were in accordance with what the Old Testament predicted about a human Messiah reigning over a restored kingdom of Israel, and Israel only, a kingdom of peace and righteousness. The Jews believed the Messiah was sent for them, the Israelites, and them alone. To them, the Messiah was a human figure, not a Divine being, but an earthly king, from the royal line of David, sent by God to lead them to freedom from Roman rule and oppression.

And, as will become clear, the Gospel of Paul was in stark contrast to the Gospel of Jesus.

Writing thirty years after the death of Jesus, Paul refers to "*my Gospel*", the Gospel "*that I preach*" and the Gospel "*which I teach in the churches everywhere*" (1 Corinthians 4:17), to differentiate it from what was being proclaimed by the remaining disciples of Jesus in the Jerusalem Church.

In Paul's teachings, as will also become clear, the human Jewish Messiah meant for the Jews only, became a Divine saviour of all nations. For Paul, Jesus was a God, a deity, and a human sacrifice, dying on the cross to atone for the sins of mankind:

"As for us, we proclaim the crucified Christ, a message that is offensive to the Jews and nonsense to the Gentiles; but for those whom God has called, both Jews and Gentiles, this message is Christ, who is the power of God and the wisdom of God". (1

Corinthians 1:23-24)

These two diverse Gospels caused great animosity between Paul and the original apostles, an animosity that, despite attempts in the Acts to disguise, is still very obvious.

In 70 C.E. Jerusalem was destroyed by the Romans. The destruction was so complete, that Josephus, the Jewish historian writing at that time, describes how it was impossible to now imagine that any people had ever lived there. The Jewish followers of Jesus, '*The followers of The Way',* were scattered or persecuted. Now there was no opposition to the Gospel of Paul. So Paul's self-created version was incorporated into the Gospel of Jesus, in many cases supplanting it.

Why?

Because Paul was writing for a Roman audience, a Roman Empire that saw Paul's teachings as being more attractive than the more stringent teachings of Jesus, based on the Jewish Torah, with its strict laws on circumcision, for example, and on what food should and should not be eaten.

Roman authorities who acknowledged that, despite three hundred years of persecution, the Christians were still increasing in numbers!

The Roman Emperor Constantine, who, in the early fourth century, decided to make this new Christian religion the religion of the Roman Empire, for political reasons, and political reasons only!

When Paul changed Jesus from the Jewish "*son of David*", sitting on David's throne, ruling a free Israel, restored to its former power and glory, to Paul's own idea of Jesus as a Divine "*Son of God*", sitting on his heavenly throne, it became necessary to invent a God-like biography for him. Thus the manifestation of the Virgin Birth, the miracles, the Resurrection, and all the other wondrous and amazing feats that the Gospels have attributed to Jesus!

And it was this, Paul's version, that found its way into the foundations of the new religion of Christianity!

Who was Paul?

Paul, the self-proclaimed apostle!

The thirteenth apostle who, in fact, as we shall see, opposed the other twelve apostles!

Paul, who never knew or never even met Jesus, about whom he professes to know so much!

Paul, who only first appears on the scene thirty years after the death of Jesus!

Paul, who claimed that he, and he only, had secret knowledge divulged and revealed to him through visions and visitations of the risen Christ!

Paul, who claimed that his "*Call to be an apostle did not come from human beings or by human means, but from Jesus Christ and God the Father, who raised him from death*". (Galatians 1:1)

Paul, who, in his own words, saw Jesus, not as a human figure, but a Divine being, raised from death by God the Father.

Paul, who was appointed '*apostle to the Gentiles'* during the split that erupted between Paul and the remaining apostles of Jesus after Jesus' death!

And why was he appointed as such?

Simply because he could get no recruits from amongst the followers of Jesus, and so had to look elsewhere, to those who had never heard Jesus preach and had never known the teachings of Judaism.

We know that Paul was originally known as Saul of Tarsus.

In his letter to the Romans, Paul himself says: "*I myself am an Israelite, a descendant of Abraham, a member of the tribe of Benjamin."* (Romans 11: 1)

And again: *"I was circumcised when I was a week old. I am an Israelite by birth, of the tribe of Benjamin, a pure-blooded Hebrew. As far as keeping the Jewish Law is concerned, I was a Pharisee, and I was so zealous that I persecuted the church."* (Philippians 3:5)

So here we see Paul very determined to make himself known as a Jew.

And not only that, but also as a Pharisee!

And telling us that he persecuted the followers of '*The Way*'.

The Pharisees, as we shall see in a later chapter, were the teachers of the Torah and of sacred scriptures, interpreting the various meanings for the Jewish people. They were the custodians, the keepers of the Law, engaging in constant friendly, amicable discussions amongst each other about the various possible interpretations, all with the view to assisting the Jewish people in applying the Law in the best way to live a good life.

So Paul has taken the trouble to make himself appear as a Pharisee.

And being a Pharisee means he must have been a Jew!

Right?

But we know how sacred the Sabbath was to the Jews! And Paul devalued the Sabbath!

"Some people think that a certain day is more important than any other days, while others think that all days are the same. We should each firmly make up our own minds." (Romans 14:5)

So, we ask, what sort of a Jew was Paul?

The dots just do not join up!

The figures just do not tally!

The jig-saw pieces just do not fit!

In his first letter to the Corinthians, Paul writes:

"I am a free man, nobody's slave; but I make myself everybody's slave in order to win as many people as possible. While working with the Jews, I live like a Jew in order to win them; and even though I myself am not subject to the Law of Moses, I live as though I were when working with those who are, in order to win them. In the same way, when working with Gentiles, I live like a Gentile, outside the Jewish Law, in order to win Gentiles. This does not mean that I don't obey God's law. Among the weak in faith I become weak like one of them, in order to win them. So I become all things to all people, that I may save some of them by whatever means are possible". (1 Corinthians 9:19-22)

A Machiavellian Paul! A Paul who ingratiates himself with whoever necessary to get what he wants!

Being born in Tarsus, Paul would have been well linked into the Hellenistic myths and religious cults.

'*Hellas*' was the ancient Greek name for what is now called Greece. What we call the '*Hellenistic Period*' in history is the period covering the history of the ancient Greek and Mediterranean worlds between the death of Alexander the Great in 323 B.C.E., and the emergence of the Roman Empire as signified by the Battle of Actium in 31 B.C.E., and the subsequent conquest of Ptolemaic Egypt (Egypt ruled by the Ptolemaic dynasty 323-30 B.C.E.) the following year.

At this time, Greek cultural influence and power was at its peak in Europe, with Africa and Asia experiencing prosperity and progress in the arts, exploration, literature, theatre, architecture, music, mathematics, philosophy and science. It is often considered a period of transition, sometimes even of decadence or degeneration, compared to the enlightenment of the Greek Classical era which preceded it, in the fifth and fourth centuries B.C.E.

The term '*Hellenistic Religion*' is the term applied to any of the various beliefs and practices of the peoples who lived under the influence of ancient Greek culture and the Hellenistic period of the Roman Empire, extended by some scholars to 33 C.E.

And the important thing to remember about Paul is that he was a product of this Hellenistic period, deeply embedded in the Roman and Greek myths associated with their deities and gods. Paul grew up on a diet of such religious cults and religions!

And, ironically, Tarsus was the very place where the Roman cult of the God Mithras had its origins!

And how would the remaining disciples and followers of Jesus have viewed this new comer? How would they have viewed this new comer who was distorting and changing what they themselves knew from actually having accompanied Jesus on his ministry?

And what would Jesus have thought about Paul?

Paul who deified Jesus and made him into a God figure, something which Jesus never ever said he was or thought of himself as!

So let us now take a look at the letters written by Paul!

The teachings of Paul

Paul certainly and obviously has a sense of his own uniqueness and self-importance, displayed constantly throughout his letters.

We see too, a very didactic Paul, a very narcissistic Paul, a very delusional Paul.

And a neurotic Paul, who would indeed make an interesting case study for a modern day psychologist or psychiatrist!

Add to this his boastfulness, his arrogance, his patronising and condescending attitude, and he certainly would not top the poll in the personality or popularity charts!

Paul proclaimed himself an apostle of Jesus, whom he never knew or even met. And on what was this self-proclamation founded?

"Am I not an apostle? Haven't I seen Jesus our Lord? And aren't you the result of my work for the Lord? Even if others do not accept me as an apostle, surely you do! Because of your life in union with the Lord, you yourselves are proof of the fact that I am an apostle". (1 Corinthians 9:1-2)

So it was in one of his many visions that he became an apostle of Jesus!

This is a recurring theme of Paul's, that Jesus selected him specifically to reveal his teachings:

"The authority that the Lord has given me." (2 Corinthians 13:10)

"For I received from the Lord the teachings that I passed on to you". (1 Corinthians 11:23)

Then, when his self-proclaimed status as an apostle of Jesus is questioned or challenged, he becomes aggressive and threatening:

"This is now the third time that I am coming to visit you. 'Any accusation must be upheld by the evidence of two or more witnesses' - as the scripture says. I want you to say to those who have sinned in the past, and to all the others; I said it before during my second visit to you, but I will say it again now that I am away; the next time I come nobody will escape punishment. You will have all the proof you want that Christ speaks through me." (2 Corinthians 13:1-3)

"I am sending you Timothy...... he will remind you of the principles which I follow in the new life in union with Christ Jesus and which I teach in all the churches everywhere. Some of you have become proud because you thought that I would not be coming to visit you. If the Lord is willing, however, I will come to you soon, and then I will find out for myself the power these proud people have, and not just what they say. For the Kingdom of God is not a matter of words but of power. Which do you prefer? Shall I come to you with a whip, or in the spirit of love and gentleness?" (1 Corinthians 4:14-21)

"As for the other matters, I will settle them when I come". (1 Corinthians 11:34)

Notice the constant use of the first person narrative ***"I"!***

Egotistical Paul!

Paul establishing his own self-importance!

Watch out everyone! Knees shaking, no doubt!

And all this from a neurotic delusionist!

A man who obviously has some sort of inner conflict going on!

"We know that the Law is spiritual; but I am unspiritual, sold as a slave to sin. I do not understand what I do; for I don't do what I would like to do, but instead I do what I hate. Since what I do is what I don't want to do, this shows that I agree that the Law is right. So I am not really the one who does this thing; rather it is the sin that lives in me - I know that good does not live in me - that is, in my human nature. For even though the desire to do good is in me, I am not able to do it. I don't do the good I want to do; instead I do the evil I don't want to do. If I do what I don't want to do, this means I am no longer the one who does it; instead it is the sin that lives in me." (Romans 7:14-20)

What sort of reverse psychology is that?

Obviously, a greatly disturbed Paul!

Even a psychotic Paul!

"*We wanted to return to you. I myself tried to go back more than once, but Satan would not let me*". (1 Thessalonians 2:18)

"But to keep me being puffed up with pride because of the many wonderful things I saw, I was given a painful physical ailment, which acts as Satan's messenger to beat me and keep me from

being proud". (2 Corinthians 12:7)

Paul, who believes he has been set upon by Satan or some other evil entity, to punish him for his boastfulness!

What boastfulness?

"But since there are so many who boast for merely human reasons, I will do the same.............But if anyone dares to boast about something........I will do the same." (2 Corinthians 11:18)

"I thank God that I speak in strange tongues more than any of you". (1 Corinthians 14:18)

"For I am not ashamed even if I have boasted somewhat too much about the authority that the Lord has given us." (2 Corinthians 10:8)

"........But I am a better servant than they are! I have worked much harder, I have been in prison more times, I have been whipped much more, and I have been near death more often." (2 Corinthians, 11: 23)

"Let no one give me any more trouble, because the scars that I have on my body show that I am the slave of Jesus." (Galatians 6:17)

And in an indirect reference to himself:

"I have to boast, even though it doesn't do any good. But I will now talk about visions and revelations given me by the Lord. I know a certain Christian man who fourteen years ago was snatched up to

the highest heaven. (I do not know whether this actually happened or whether it was a vision - only God knows), and there he heard things that cannot be put into words, things that human lips may not speak. So I will boast about this man....." (2 Corinthians 12:1-5)

Here he obviously believed he was transported up to heaven!

Something for him to boast about!

But, reality check! Delusional or what?

On the other hand, he warns against boasting:

"Nobody is going to turn my rightful boast into empty words! have no right to boast just because I preach the gospel. After all, I am under orders to do so". (1 Corinthians 9:16)

"This means that no one can boast in God's presence". (1 Corinthians 1:29)

He even tells his followers:

"Do not allow yourselves to be condemned by anyone who claims to be superior because of special visions and who insists on false humility.......For no reason at all, such people are all puffed up by their human way of thinking and have stopped holding on to Christ". (2 Colossians 2:18-19)

Talk about not being able to see the wood for the trees! Or not seeing the splinter in your own eye!

A totally delusional Paul!

And what about his arrogance?

"Actually I would prefer that all of you were as I am..." (1 Corinthians 7:7)

"Imitate me then, just as I imitate Christ". (1 Corinthians 11:1)

Jesus, whom he never even met!

What about his patronising and condescending?

*"When I came to you, my brothers and sisters, to preach God's secret truth, I did not use big words and great learning". (*1 Corinthians 2:1)

*"Now remember what you were , my brothers and sisters, when God called you. From the human point of view, few of you were wise or powerful or of high social standing. God purposely chose what the world considers nonsense in order to shame the wise, and he chose what the world considers weak in order to shame the powerful. He chose what the world looks down on and despises, and thinks is nothing, in order to destroy what the world thinks is important." (*1 Corinthians 1:26-28)

"There is a secret truth, my brothers and sisters, which I want you to know, for it will keep you from thinking how wise you are". (Romans 11: 25)

We see a didactic, even an admonishing Paul:

"If any of you have a dispute with another Christian, how dare you

*go before heathen judges instead of letting God's people settle the matter?........Do you know that we shall judge the angels? How much more, then the things of this life! If such matters come up, are you going to take them to be settled by people who have no standing in the church? Shame on you!" (*1 Corinthians 6:1-5)

"You must teach and preach these things. Whoever teaches a different doctrine and does not agree with the true words of our Lord Jesus Christ and with the teaching of our religion, is swollen with pride and knows nothing". (1 Timothy 6:3-4)

"Now it is actually being said that there is sexual immorality among you so terrible that not even the heathen would be guilty of it. I am told there is a man sleeping with his stepmother!.....I have in the name of our Lord Jesus Christ already passed judgement on the man who has done this terrible thing. As you meet together, and I meet with you in my spirit, by the power of our Lord Jesus present with us, you are to hand this man over to Satan for his body to be destroyed, so that his spirit may be saved in the Day of the Lord." (1 Corinthians: 5:1-6)

"In the letter that I wrote to you, I told you not to associate with immoral people. Now I did not mean pagans who are immoral or greedy or are thieves or who worship idols. To avoid them you would have to get out of the world completely. What I meant was that you should not associate with a person who calls himself a believer but is immoral or greedy or worships idols or is a slanderer or a drunkard or a thief. Don't even sit down to eat with such a person." (1 Corinthians 5:9-11)

Here is a very judgemental Paul, but again, a Paul who is deluding himself:

"After all, it is none of my business to judge outsiders. God will judge them. But should you not judge the members of your own fellowship? As the scripture says, 'Remove the evil person from your group.' " (1 Corinthians 5:12-13)

Surely you know that the wicked will not possess God's Kingdom? Do not fool yourselves; people who are immoral or who worship false idols or are adulterers or homosexual perverts or who steal or are greedy or are drunkards or who slander others or are thieves - none of these will possess God's Kingdom. Some of you were like that. But you have been purified from sin..." (1 Corinthians 6:9-11)

And what has Paul got to say on women, marriage and celibacy?

Ready for this?

"The man who marries does well, but the man who does not marry does even better". (1 Corinthians 7:38)

"A man does well not to marry". (1 Corinthians 7:1)

"An unmarried man concerns himself with the Lord's work, because he is trying to please the Lord. But a married man concerns himself with worldly matters, because he wants to please his wife, and so he is pulled in two directions..... An unmarried woman or virgin concerns herself with the Lord's work, because she wants to be dedicated both in body and spirit; but a married woman concerns herself with worldly matters, because she wants to please her husband. I am saying this because I want to help you. I am not trying to put restriction on you. Instead, I want you to do what is right and proper, and to give yourselves completely to the Lord's service without any reservation." (1 Corinthians 7:32-35)

"Now, to the unmarried and to the widows I say that it would be better for you to continue to live alone as I do. But if you cannot restrain your desires, go ahead and marry - it is better to marry than to burn with passion." (1 Corinthians 7:7-9)

"I would rather spare you the everyday troubles that married people will have........ there is not much time left........and from now on married men should live as though they were not married..........for this world, as it is now, will not last much longer." (1 Corinthians 7:28-31)

"A married woman is not free as long as her husband lives; but if her husband dies, then she is free to be married to any man she wishes, but only if he is a Christian. She will be happier, however, if she stays as she is. That is my opinion, and I think that I too have God's Spirit." (1 Corinthians 7:39-40)"

"The husband is supreme over his wife, and God is supreme over Christ. So a man who prays or proclaims God's message in public worship with his head covered disgraces Christ. And any woman who prays or proclaims God's message in public worship with nothing on her head disgraces her husband; there is no difference between her and a woman whose head has been shaved. If the woman does not cover her head, she might as well cut her hair. And since it is a shameful thing for a woman to shave her head or cut her hair, she should cover her head. A man has no need to cover his head, because he reflects the image and glory of man; for a man was not created from woman, but woman from man. Nor was man created for woman's sake, but woman was created for man's sake. On account of the angels, then, a woman should have a covering over her head to show that she is under her husband's authority". (1 Corinthians 11:2-10)

"As in all the churches of God's people, the women should keep quiet in the meetings.......... If they want to find out about something, they should ask their husbands at home. It is a disgraceful thing for a woman to speak in church." (1 Corinthians 14: 34-35)

"In every church service I want the men to pray, men who are dedicated to God and can lift up their hands in prayer without anger or argument. I also want the women to be modest and sensible about their clothes and to dress properly; not with fancy hair styles or with gold ornaments or pearls or expensive dresses, but with good deeds, as is proper for women who claim to be religious. Women should learn in silence and all humility. I do not allow them to teach or to have authority over men, they must keep quiet. For Adam was created first, and then Eve. And it was not Adam who was deceived; it was the woman who was deceived and broke God's law." (1 Timothy 2:8-15)

"Nature itself teaches you that long hair on a man is a disgrace, but on a woman it is a thing of beauty. Her long hair has been given her to serve as a covering". (1 Corinthians 11:14-15)

Did Jesus not have long hair? The style worn by Jewish men, with a parting in the centre, locks flowing freely down each side?

Now let us consider Paul as an agent of the Romans!

Their very own propaganda machine!

"Everyone must obey the state authorities, because no authority exists without God's permission and the existing authorities have been put there by God. Whoever opposes the existing authority

opposes what God has ordered, and anyone who does so will bring judgement on himself. For rulers are not to be feared by those who do good, but by those who do evil. Would you like to be unafraid of those in authority? Then do what is good, and they will praise you, because they are God's servants working for your own good. But if you do evil, then be afraid of them, because their power to punish is real. They are God's servants and carry out God's punishment on those who do evil. For this reason you must obey the authorities - not just because of God's punishment, but also as a matter of conscience.

That is also why you pay taxes, because the authorities are working for God when they fulfil their duties. Pay, then, what you owe them; pay them your personal and property taxes, and show respect and honour for them all." (Romans 13:1-7)

Taxation!

The main source of unrest and hatred for the Jewish people!

The burden of taxation imposed upon them by the Roman authorities was the main reason that sparked off most of the Jewish uprisings!

And here is Paul telling them to pay their taxes!

Paul, the Roman! Ingratiating himself with the Roman authorities!

No wonder the early Christian Roman Church adopted Paul's teachings!

It suited them perfectly to do so!

Free propaganda!

Good old Paul!

Paul who will keep order for us!

And what has Paul got to say on slavery?

Slavery! So prominent throughout the Roman Empire!

"Slaves, obey your human masters with fear and trembling, and do so with a sincere heart, as though you were serving Christ. Do this not only when they are watching you, because you want to gain their approval, but with all your heart do what God wants, as slaves of Christ. Do your work as slaves cheerfully, as though you served the Lord, and not merely human beings. Remember that the Lord will reward everyone, whether slave or free, for the good work they do." (Ephesians 6:5-8)

"Those who are slaves must consider their masters worthy of all respect, so that no one will speak evil of the name of God and of our teaching. Slaves belonging to Christian masters must not despise them, for they are their brothers and sisters. Instead, they are to serve them even better, because those who benefit from their work are believers whom they love." (1 Timothy 6:1-2)

Talk about brain-washing, propaganda and spin!

Paul! The Roman propaganda machine!

Even his teachings on vegetarianism must have been sweet music to Roman ears!

"Some people's faith allows them to eat anything, but the person who is weak in the faith eats only vegetables.......... You then, who eat only vegetables - why do you pass judgement on others? And you who eat anything - why do you despise other believers?...........My union with the Lord Jesus makes me certain that no food is of itself ritually unclean......." (Romans 14:2-3; 10:14)

What else would early Christian Church leaders have welcomed from Paul?

"When people criticise me, this is how I defend myself: Haven't I the right to be given food and drink for my work? Haven't I the right to follow the example of the other apostles and the Lord's brothers and Peter and, by taking a Christian wife with me on my travels?.........We have sown spiritual seed among you. Is it too much if we reap material benefit from you? If others have the right to expect this from you, haven't we an even greater right?...... Surely you know that the men who work in the Temple get their food from the Temple and that those who offer the sacrifices on the altar get a share of the sacrifices. In the same way, the Lord has ordered that those who preach the gospel should get their living from it............ " (1 Corinthians 9:3-14)

The Roman Catholic Church has adopted this!

And here we also learn that Jesus not only had brothers, but that they were amongst his apostles, and they were married!

And their wives accompanied them on their travels with Jesus!

"In the church God has put all in place: in the first place apostles. In

the second place prophets, and in the third place teachers; then those who perform miracles, followed by those who are given the power to heal or to help others or to direct them or to speak in strange tongues. They are not all apostles or prophets or teachers". (12: 28-29)

A hierarchy in the Church!

Something, surely, which Jesus never advocated!

But which the Roman Catholic Church does! Big time!

We have seen how the early Church fathers changed the order of the writings in the New Testament to make it appear that Paul's writings came after the Gospels, rather than before.

That means that the Gospels must have got their inspiration from Paul!

Right?

So, let us look at just a few of the teachings of Paul that found their way into the Gospels!

"I passed on to you what I received which is of the greatest importance: that Christ died for our sins, as written in the Scriptures; that he was buried and that he was raised to life three days later, as written in the Scriptures; that he appeared to Peter and then to all twelve apostles. Then he appeared to more than 500 of his followers at once, most of whom are still, alive, although some have died. Then he appeared to James, and afterwards to all the apostles.

Last of all he appeared also to me........" (1 Corinthians 15:3-8)

Obviously Paul's visions again! Jesus was already dead thirty years before Paul came on the scene!

"*The Day of the Lord will come as a thief comes at night. When people say, 'Everything is quiet and safe', then suddenly destruction will hit them!"* (1 Thessalonians 5:2-3)

"*... when the Lord Jesus appears from heaven with his mighty angels, with a flaming fire, to punish those who reject God and who do not obey the Good News about our Lord Jesus. They will suffer the punishment of eternal destruction, separated from the presence of the Lord and from his glorious might, when he comes on that day to receive glory from all who believe".* (2 Thessalonians 1: 7-10)

Obviously the Gospels were influenced by Paul!

And that was what the early Church fathers were so desperately trying to hide!

The chief cause of the rift between the remaining followers of Jesus after his death and Paul was the nature of Paul's teachings regarding the Divinity of Jesus:

"God did not even keep back his own Son, but offered him for us all! He gave us his Son........Christ Jesus, who died, or rather, was raised to life and is at the right side of God, pleading with him for us!" (Romans 8:32-34)

"Now that we have been put right with God through faith, we have

peace with God through our Lord Jesus Christ.......it was while we were still sinners that Christ died for us! By his blood we are now put right with God........We were God's enemies, but he made us his friends through the death of his Son." (Romans 5:1-10)

"If you confess that Jesus is Lord and believe that God raised him from death, you will be saved. For it is by our faith that we are put right with God". (Romans 10:9)

"For the Gospel reveals how God puts people right with himself: it is through faith from beginning to end. As the scripture says, 'The person who is put right with God through faith shall live'." (Romans 1: 17)

"God made peace through his Son's blood on the cross and so brought back to himself all things, both on earth and in heaven.........but now by the physical death of his Son, God has made you his friends......It is this Gospel that I, Paul, became a servant - this Gospel which has been preached to everybody in the world". (Colossians 1:20-23)

"If Christ has not been raised from death, then we have nothing to preach and you have nothing to believe." (1 Corinthians 15:14)

"For I received from the Lord the teaching that I passed on to you: that the Lord Jesus, on the night he was betrayed, took a piece of bread, gave thanks to God, broke it, and said, 'This is my body, which is for you. Do this in memory of me.' In the same way, after the supper, he took the cup and said, ' This cup is God's new covenant, sealed with my blood. Whenever you drink it, do so in memory of me'." (1 Corinthians 11:23-25)

So it was these teachings of Paul concerning the Divinity of Jesus and faith alone being the requisite for salvation that led to the rift between Paul and the remaining followers of Jesus.

Paul tells us about this rift in Galatians, including the words he had with Peter:

"But those who seemed to be the leaders - I say this because it makes no difference to me what they were; God does not judge by outward appearances - those leaders, I say, made no new suggestions to me. On the contrary, they saw that God had given me the task of preaching the gospel to the Gentiles, just as he had given Peter the task of preaching the gospel to the Jews. For by God's power I was made an apostle to the Gentiles, just as Peter was made an apostle to the Jews. James, Peter, and John, who seemed to be the leaders, recognized that God had given me this special task; so they shook hands with Barnabas and me, as a sign that we were all partners. We agreed that Barnabas and I would work with the Gentiles and they among the Jews." (Galatians 2:6-9)

Then he continues:

"But when Peter came to Antioch, I opposed him in public, because he was clearly wrong. Before some men who had been sent by James arrived there, Peter had been eating with the Gentile brothers and sisters. But after these men arrived, he drew back and would not eat with the Gentiles, because he was afraid of those who were in favour of circumcising them. The other Jewish brothers and sisters also started acting like cowards along with Peter, and even Barnabas, was swept along by their cowardly action. When I saw that they were not walking a straight path in line with the

truth of the gospel, I said to Peter in front of them all, ' You are a Jew, yet you have been living like a Gentile, not like a Jew. How then can you try to force Gentiles to live like Jews?" (Galatians 2: 11-14)

And all this tirade from a man who, we saw earlier, proclaimed to be all things to all people, being a Jew or a Gentile or whatever, according to the dictates of the moment!

Paul's self-righteousness combined, this time, with his arrogance!

In Ephesians we read:

"God revealed his secret plan and made it known to me.........in past times human beings were not told this secret, but God has revealed it now by the Spirit to his holy apostles and prophets .The secret is that by means of the gospel the Gentiles have a part with the Jews in God's blessings; they are members of the same body and share in the promise that God made through Christ Jesus." (Ephesians 3:3-6)

And again, in Galatians:

"*So there is no difference between Jews and Gentiles, between slaves and free people, between men and women; you are all one in union with Christ Jesus*". (Galatians *3:28)*

Here we have a Paul who is turning the old established economic principle that demand creates supply on its head!

Paul is promoting himself as the person who will bring the Gospel to the Gentiles; he will supply the means, the secret disclosed to only him, by God, which he will reveal to the Gentiles. So, having him to preach to them they will not lose out on the fact that Jesus did not get round to them when he was alive. They have Paul now!

Talk about creating a job for yourself!

And selling it!

And his legacy lives on!

So, what can we conclude from our analysis of the Pauline letters?

Surely we can conclude the following:

- Paul's letters, though the first of the New Testament writings, have been placed ***after*** the Gospels by the early Church fathers! Obviously, to disguise the fact that the writers of the Gospels were influenced heavily by Paul's writings!
- Paul never knew or even met Jesus!
- Paul claimed that all his knowledge came from secret revelations to him personally from the risen Jesus.
- Paul proclaimed himself an apostle as a result of one of these visions.
- Paul, in his writings, comes across as delusional, narcissistic, egotistical, didactic, admonishing, domineering, patronising, arrogant, condescending, judgemental, boastful and tolerating no opposition.
- Paul was obviously intending to ingratiate himself with the Roman authorities, with his pro-Roman teachings and propaganda.
- Paul's teachings differed greatly from those of Jesus. Jesus

nowhere suggests that he saw himself as a deity, but only as a human Messiah, and a Messiah for the Jews only. Paul, on the other hand, saw Jesus as a human sacrifice, dying on the cross for the sins of mankind.

- Paul taught that faith was all important for salvation, in fact, the only requisite for salvation. Jesus, on the other hand, taught that good actions and repentance were necessary for salvation.
- It was Paul's teachings that caused the rift between Paul and the remaining followers of Jesus.
- Nowhere in his writings does Paul mention his alleged conversion on the road to Damascus! The very thing that most people know about him! Does that mean it never actually happened! Was it made up by Luke in Acts to highlight the change in Paul by contrast?
- Paul claimed to be a Jew and a Pharisee. Yet in his work as persecuting the Jewish followers of Jesus, he was in the police force of the Sadducees, the bitter enemies of the Pharisees!
- Paul's writings obviously influenced the Gospels.
- Paul deified and mythologised Jesus according to his own Hellenistic background, complete with Gods and Goddesses, sacrificial flesh and blood, atonement to appease an angry God. To compete with such as this, Jesus needed to be deified and be seen to accomplish the same supernatural feats the other Gods were accomplishing.
- Paul makes virtually no mention of anything Jesus did or said while alive. Nor does he mention the virgin birth or any of the miracles other than the Resurrection.

Why not? Because he was not interested in the teachings of Jesus.

Paul was only interested in Paul's teachings! His teachings did not adhere to the teachings of Jesus or his apostles!

- For the same reason, he does not mention the Beautitudes or any of the parables of Jesus.

Now, finally, let us take a look at the bigger picture!

Paul was a Pharisee who freely admitted that he taught by revelation.

Paul ended up in Rome, and we now have the Roman Catholic Church, which bears a remarkable resemblance to Paul's church structure!

Paul's teachings about being saved by faith alone is the corner stone of the Catholic Church! Believe, believe, believe is their constant message!

Don't question! Just believe!

Faith! The ultimate word for the Church apologists! There is no argument against it! Have faith!

At the Council of Nicaea in 325 C.E., this same Church chose to include no less than thirteen of Paul's letters into their biblical canon!

And this at the same time as they left out other written Gospels!

After all, Paul's writings were not called the '*Pauline Doctrine*' for no reason!

And it was the writings of this man Paul which were included in the teachings of early Christianity!

Writings which excluded anything about the life or teachings of Jesus!

The dots just do not join up!

The figures just do not tally!

The jig-saw pieces just do not fit!

And that's the Gospel truth!

Chapter 4:

The Canonical Gospels in the New Testament

One of the main arguments the Church has always put forward for the authenticity of the Gospels is that they were written by eyewitnesses of the events described and narrated. We have been led to believe that they were written by Matthew, Mark, Luke and John, the actual disciples of Jesus, who accompanied him in his ministry, and that they must therefore, be considered as primary and reliable evidence.

But we have already established that these four canonical Gospels were written at the end of the first century C.E., about 35 to 65 years after the actual death of Jesus. The authors were not eye-witnesses to the ministry of Jesus, and they cannot, therefore, be considered as either primary or reliable evidence.

Mark was, allegedly, the later companion of the disciple Peter, so he would have heard second-hand about Jesus, from Peter.

Luke was a companion of Paul, who, as we have just seen, was not even around when Jesus was performing his ministry. So Luke is even further removed from Jesus than was Mark.

We have also established that the authors are unknown, simply writing in the names of Matthew, Mark, Luke and John. These Gospels are what is called '*pseudo-biographical*' works, a common feature amongst early writers, where the author was writing from the view point of another, using a pseudo name.

A second main argument in support of the authenticity of the Gospels is that they are all independent of each other.

Well, this is not true either!

Contrary to what we have been led to believe, and as already explained, it was Mark's Gospel that was written first, in about 71 C.E., shortly after the death by crucifixion, of the Apostle Peter in 67 C.E., and reflecting Peter's understanding of the teachings and life of Jesus.

So the Gospel of Mark is the first narrative we have of the life of Jesus, written just after 70 C.E.

But remember! Mark would have had knowledge of the writings of Paul in the Pauline letters, as Paul was writing previous to him, about 50-60 C.E.

Matthew's Gospel was written second, about 80-85

So Matthew would have had Mark's Gospel as reference. And not just as a reference, as we shall see! In fact, Matthew mostly repeats Mark, and in many cases, word for word!

So we cannot say that these are independent accounts!

Thirdly, we have the Gospel of Luke, written 85-90 A.D.

Luke acknowledges the works of others in his very first words, expressly stating that he knows of earlier written accounts of the life of Jesus: "*Dear Theophilus: Many people have done their best to write a report of the things that have taken place among us.*

They wrote what we have been told by those who saw these things from the beginning and who proclaimed the message. And so, Your Excellency, because I have carefully studied all these matters from their beginning, I thought it would be good to write an orderly account for you. I do this so that you will know the full truth about everything which you have been taught."

General opinion agrees that Theophilus was a high ranking official of the Roman authorities.

And is Luke actually suggesting here that the former writers did not write "*an orderly account*", so is he, Luke himself, now going to do it?

He certainly takes a lot from both Mark and Matthew, adding in bits and pieces of his own.

Again, this means that Luke is not an independent source either!

And certainly, when we see just to what a great extent they borrow or copy from each other, then it is very obvious that they cannot be considered independent sources.

Finally, we have the fourth Gospel, that of John, written approximately 90 to 100 C.E., which deviates greatly from the previous three, so much so that we hardly recognise this Jesus from the Jesus of the previous three.

John depicts a Divine Jesus, part of the Godhead, an eternal being, an exalted Son of God. This is in direct contrast to how the disciples of Jesus saw him, those who actually accompanied him on his ministry. To them Jesus was the promised Messiah, a human being, not a deity or in any way Divine, but a human Messiah, the human King of the House of David, the saviour sent by God to free the Israeli people from Roman rule.

How can we explain this vast difference?

One very possible explanation lies in the fact that Jesus in the first three Gospels is an apocalyptic Jesus, prophesising that the end time would come in his own life-time.

Then, when it did not come, the writers had to change their story!

Hence, John's Gospel has a completely different focus and emphasis.

Furthermore, in John's Gospel there are only seven miracles reported, in contrast to the more numerous miracles in the synoptics, where the purpose of these miracles is to present evidence to support the claim that Jesus is the true Messiah. The evidence for this claim rests on Jesus' ability to do that which ordinary human beings cannot do.

Only two of the Gospels, that of Matthew and that of Luke, show any interest at all in the birth and early years of Jesus. Mark and John, on the other hand, show a distinct lack of concern about the life of Jesus before the actual start of his ministry, which began when he was thirty years old.

Mark, indeed does not even mention the Resurrection either. His focus is totally on the ministry.

A further arguement put forward is that the Gospels were all written at different times and in different places.

Well, yes, they were written at different times, but that does not negate the fact that they most certainly cannot be assessed as four independent sources! This has been acknowledged, indeed, by the very fact that the first three together, that of Mark, Matthew and Luke, are known, as we have seen earlier, as the '*Synoptic Gospels*' due to the close similarities between them!

Probably the main test for any historian is the criterion of multiple attestation, which means that when two or more independent sources present similar or consistent accounts, then that story is much more likely to prove authentic. But the operative and crucial words here are the words '*independent*' and '*consistent*'.

And these Gospels are neither independent nor consistent! Rather, they are, ironically, both synoptic and contradictory!

Such a great number of contradictions in stories that are common to all of them, plus so many events that are unique to one or other Gospel, leads the reader to accept that yes, there is a serious problem about authenticity!

The only two events that most scholars agree are authentic are the Baptism of Jesus by John the Baptiser, and the Crucifixion of Jesus by the order of the Roman Prefect Pontius Pilate. And even certain details about the Crucifixion raise serious questions. Much more in dispute are the two narratives about the Birth of Jesus, and the miraculous events surrounding, for example, the Resurrection and the Ascension.

And, as we read through these four canonical Gospels, indeed, we can see they all have a common agenda! They were all obviously written with the purpose of glorifying Jesus!

And knowing the purpose for which they were written certainly aids the reader in the detection of bias!

So we must ask the obvious question! Why were the writers of the Gospels intent in glorifying Jesus? Why did they attribute to him the qualities of a deity, and not a human person? Why did they have him perform miracles and wondrous deeds, which other mortal men cannot do?

Jesus and his earliest followers were Jewish, firmly embedded in the teachings of the Jewish Torah. They knew nothing about any later Church doctrines, Christian dogma or teachings. Jesus and his earliest followers were not Christians! They were Jews!

Jesus did not come to found a Church or a new religion! He was the Messiah to the Jewish people! And only the Jewish people!

His teachings were from the Torah, not from any Christian teachings or dogma!

So why have the writers of the Gospels portrayed Jesus in the way in which they have done?

In chapter 6 we will be looking at each of the main events in the life of Jesus, as related in the Canonical Gospels, and see what conclusions we can reach about the way in which Jesus is portrayed!

CHAPTER 5:

THE 'ACTS OF THE APOSTLES' IN THE NEW TESTAMENT

The Acts of the Apostles is a continuation of the Gospel of Luke.

And as the continuation of the Gospel of Luke, we can expect to find the usual plethora of contradictions, distortions and manipulations that we have found permeating the other Gospels!

And we are not disappointed in our expectations!

The chief purpose of Acts is to tell how Jesus' early followers, led by the Holy Spirit, spread the Good News about him *"in Jerusalem, in all Judea and Samaria, and to the ends of the earth". (Acts 1:8)*

So it depicts the story of the spread of Christianity, with the emphasis diverted from apocalyptic expectations to more earthly concerns.

It also depicts the growing distance between Christianity and Judaism, and the triumph of the Christian message despite persecutions.

And more importantly, it also attempts to disguise the rift between Paul and the other remaining disciples of Jesus!

But again, the holes are there!

Luke! An admirer and follower of Paul!

The admiration was obviously mutual, as Paul describes Luke as "*Our dear doctor*". (Colossians 4:14)

Luke! The biographer of Paul!

And a lot of those discrepancies and contradictions have got to do with Paul.

Yes! Paul dominates here in the Acts as well!

But the Paul in Luke's Acts is very different from the self-portraiture of Paul in own his letters.

We saw in the letters a Paul who taught by revelation, a Paul who was given secret knowledge from visions and visitations from the risen Christ.

But nowhere in the Gospels is there any hint whatsoever that Jesus ever had intended doing such a thing! It is just not believable that, having spent three years with his disciples teaching them, that Jesus would wait until he was dead and suddenly start to give secret knowledge to someone else, knowledge which he never imparted to them!

In Acts, there is no mention of Paul the letter-writer, and he is not called an apostle except on one occasion:

"The people of the city (Iconium) were divided; some were for the Jews, others for the apostles. (Paul and Barnabas) (Acts 14:4)

In sharp contrast to the Paul of the letters, Luke now in Acts, creates a much more subdued, even subordinate Paul, obviously in an attempt to soften and divert attention away from the conflict between the early Christian communities of Jews and Gentiles.

Even the conflict itself has a different emphasis!

In the letters, the conflict was between Paul and the people in his communities, whereas now in Acts, the conflict is between Paul and the Jewish and Gentile authorities:

Paul, in his letter to the Corinthians, instructs his followers*: "By the authority of Our Lord Jesus Christ, I appeal to all of you, my brothers and sisters, to agree in what you say, so that there will be no divisions among you. Be completely united, with only one thought and one purpose ....for some people have told me there are quarrels among you............each one of you says something different.... I thank God I did not baptize any of you......No one can say, then, that you were baptized as my disciples....."(1* Corinthians 1:10-15)

Here we have Paul telling us about the conflict being within his own communities, whereas, in Acts, the conflict is between Paul and the authorities!

Obviously Luke trying to play down the problems in the early Church!

Paul in Acts was in conflict with his companions Barnabas and John Mark, so they left him:

"There was a sharp argument, and they separated. Barnabas took Mark and sailed off for Cyprus, while Paul chose Silas, and left.........Paul travelled to Derbe and Lystra...." (Acts 15:39-40)

We may well wonder what that was about!

It certainly was not mentioned in any of the letters! No one would have dared to oppose Paul there!

In Acts too, Paul faces antagonism, for example, in Ephesus:

"Paul went into the synagogue and during three months spoke boldly with the people, holding discussions with them and trying to convince them about the Kingdom of God. But some of them were stubborn, and would not believe, and before the whole group they said things about the Way of the Lord. So Paul left them and took the believers with him." (Acts 19:8-9)

And even Paul's teachings are different in Acts from the letters!

For example, the emphasis put by Paul on "*justification by faith*" that we read in the letters is absent from his speeches and sermons in Acts.

The greatest bone of contention, though, was about Paul's attitude towards the Law. In contrast to Jesus' teachings, where the Law was to be observed, Paul attempted to make the Law void.

Contradictions and discrepancies abound!

For example, Paul declared all things lawful:

"So let no one make rules about what you eat or drink or about holy days or the New Moon Festival or the Sabbath." (Colossians 2:16)

Compared to Jesus' words:

"Do not think that I have come to do away with the Law of Moses and the teachings of the prophets. I have not come to do away with them, but to make their teachings come true. Remember that as long as heaven and earth last, not the least point nor the smallest detail of the Law will be done away with - not until the end of all things." (Matthew 5: 17-18)

And again, Paul declared nothing unclean:

"My union with the Lord Jesus makes me certain that no food is of itself ritually unclean, but if a person believes that some food is unclean, then it becomes unclean for that person." (Romans 14:14)

Yet:

" 'It is my opinion', James went on, 'that we should not trouble the Gentiles who are turning to God. Instead we should write a letter telling them not to eat any food that is ritually unclean because it has been offered to idols.' " (Acts 15:19-20)

Different, too, is the Jerusalem Council dealing with issues arising from Gentiles now entering the new movement:

"...we have agreed not to put any other burden on you besides these necessary rules: eat no food that has been offered to idols; eat no blood; eat no animal that has been strangled; and keep yourselves from sexual immorality. You will do well if you take care not to do these things." (Acts 15:28-29)

Compared to what we read in Paul's letters:

"We agreed that Barnabas and I would work among the Gentiles and they among the Jews. All they asked was that we should remember the needy in their group, which is the very thing I have been eager to do." (Galatians 2: 9:10)

But as we can see, Paul is lying in Galatians, as that is not what James said in Acts!

James never mentioned the poor!

Remember reading in Paul's letters how he identified himself as Saul from Tarsus, a Jew and a Pharisee?

Well, in Acts, he is also referred to as *"A man from Tarsus named Saul."* (Acts 9: 11)

And: *"I am a Jew, born in Tarsus in Cilicia, a citizen of an important city."* (Acts 22:3)

Yet in Acts 22 we read, when Paul was under arrest and threatened with whipping: *"Paul said to the officer standing there, 'Is it lawful for you to whip a Roman citizen who hasn't even been tried for any crime?'*

When the officer heard this, he went to the commander and asked him, 'What are you doing? That man is a Roman citizen.'

So the commander went to Paul and asked him, 'Tell me, are you a Roman citizen?'

'Yes,' answered Paul.

The commander said, 'I became one by paying a large amount of money.'

'But I became one by birth,' answered Paul..........And the commander was frightened when he realized that Paul was a Roman citizen and that he had put him in chains."(Acts 22:25-29)

So here we have Paul claiming to be a Roman citizen by birth!

But he cannot be both a Roman and a Pharisee!

On one of these occasions, Paul is not being truthful!

More lies!

In Acts, we read how the young Saul left Tarsus and went to Jerusalem, where he studied with the highly respected Pharisee called Gamaliel:

"I am a Jew, born in Tarsus in Cilicia, but brought up here in Jerusalem as a student of Gamaliel. I received strict instruction in the Law of our ancestors and was just as dedicated to God as are all of you who are here today. I persecuted to the death the people who followed the Way. I arrested men and women and threw them into prison. The High Priest and the whole Council can prove that I am telling the truth. I received from them letters written to fellow-Jews in Damascus, so I went there to arrest these people and bring them back to Jerusalem to be punished." (Acts 22:3-5)

Yet Paul, in his letters, never mentions Gamaliel or having studied with him!

Paul does not mention either, in his letters, about his conversion on the way to Damascus!

Such a miraculous happening, the event that allegedly changed not only his name from Saul to Paul, but changed his whole life!

But to compensate, we hear about it no less than three times in Acts!

And of course complete with contradictions!

"As Saul was coming near the city of Damascus, suddenly a bright light from the sky flashed round him. he fell to the ground and heard a voice saying to him, 'Saul, Saul! Why do you persecute me?'

'Who are you, Lord?' he said.

'I am Jesus, whom you persecute,' the voice said. 'But get up and go into the city where you will be told what you must do.'

The men who were travelling with Saul had stopped, not saying a word; they heard the voice but could not see anyone.

Saul got up from the ground and opened his eyes, but could not see a thing. So they took him by the hand and led him into Damascus. For three days he was not able to see, and during that time he did not eat or drink anything." (Acts 9:7-9)

In this account, Saul's sight was restored by Ananias, when at his touch, *"at once something like fish scales fell from Saul's eyes and he was able to see again."* (Acts 9:18)

But Paul himself gives an account of the same event twice, when he is on trial:

"Many times I had them punished in the synagogues and tried to make them deny their faith. I was so furious with them that I even went to foreign cities to persecute them.

It was for this purpose that I went to Damascus with authority from the chief priests. It was on the road at midday, Your Majesty, that I saw a light much brighter than the sun, coming from the sky and shining round me and the men travelling with me. All of us fell to the ground, and I heard a voice say to me in Hebrew, 'Saul, Saul! Why are you persecuting me? You are hurting yourself by hitting back, like an ox kicking against its owner's stick '

'Who are you, Lord?' I asked. And the Lord answered, 'I am Jesus, whom you persecute. But get up and stand on your feet. I have appeared to you to appoint you as my servant. You are to tell others what you have seen of me today and what I will show you in the future. I will rescue you from the people of Israel and from the Gentiles to whom I will send you. You are to open their eyes and turn them from the darkness to the light and from the power of Satan to God.' " (Acts 26:11-18)

No mention of blindness here!

And quite an embellishment from the first version!

Luke seems to have got carried away in the telling!

In fact, we might even ask ourselves, did it ever even happen at all?

"As I was travelling and coming near Damascus, about midday, a bright light from the sky flashed suddenly round me. I fell to the ground and heard a voive saying to me, ' Saul, Saul! Why do you persecute me?'

'Who are you, Lord?' I asked. 'I am Jesus of Nazareth, whom you persecute,' he said to me. The men with me saw the light, but did not hear the voice of the one who was speaking to me........I was blind because of the bright light, and so my companions took me by the hand and led me into Damascus." (Acts 22: 6-11)

But in the first account, we were told that the men with Paul heard the voice but could not see anyone. Now we are told that the men saw the light but heard nothing!

Furthermore, in one of his accounts, Paul received full revelation on the spot, concerning what he was supposed to do. In the other account, however, he was told to go to Damascus, where he would be told what to do.

Paul lying again!

"It was three years later that I went to Jerusalem to obtain information from Peter, and I stayed with him for two weeks. I did not see any other apostle except James, the Lord's brother.

What I write to you is true. God knows I am not lying!" (Galatians 1:18-20)

Paul obviously needs to convince people he is not lying!

And what about the word '*Christian'?*

Neither Jesus nor any of his disciples ever mentioned the word 'Christian'!

According to Acts, the disciples were first called Christians in Antioch, under the tutelage of Barnabas and Paul!

"Then Barnabas went to Tarsus to look for Saul. When he found him, he took him to Antioch, and for a whole year, the two met with the people of the church and taught a large group. It was at Antioch that the believers were first called Christians." (Acts 11:25-26)

So clearly, Christianity came from Paul's teachings, not from the teachings of Jesus!

And why not from the teachings of Jesus?

Because Jesus was a Jew! Not a Christian!

That's why!

CHAPTER 6:

THE JIG-SAW PIECES JUST DO NOT FIT!

Let us now look closely at the main events in the life of Jesus, as related in the four Canonical Gospels

The Birth of Jesus

Only two out of the four Gospels include the birth of Jesus. These are Matthew and Luke. Mark and John never even mention the birth.

We know from the Gospels that Mary was betrothed to Joseph, but before they were married, Mary became pregnant. Living in such a small closely knit community as Nazareth, this would have been widely seen as a scandal, and indeed, Luke tells us about how Mary went to stay with her relative Elizabeth*, "in the hill country of Judea*". (Luke 1:39)

"*Mary stayed about three months with Elizabeth and then went back home".* (Luke 1:56)

We can assume that this prolonged stay was probably to protect Mary from the wagging tongues!

Now, we must ask ourselves, if the birth was a virgin birth, as the Church has taught for the last 2,000 years, why do two out of the four Gospels not even mention it?

Surely such a remarkable event as the miraculous virgin birth of the Saviour would be worth including?

And what do the two writers who do mention this extraordinary event actually say about it?

What exactly do they say about this so-called '*Virgin Birth*'? This '*Virgin Birth*' that is so fundamental to the teachings of the Roman Catholic Church and so important for them to uphold?

First, Matthew writes: *"This was how the birth of Jesus took place. His mother Mary was engaged to Joseph, but before they were married, she found out that she was going to have a baby by the Holy Spirit* ". (Matthew 1:18)

There is no mention of a virgin here!

In the next line, however, Matthew writes: "*While he (Joseph) was thinking about this, an angel of the Lord appeared to him in a dream and said: Joseph, descendant of David, do not be afraid to take Mary to be your wife. For it is by the Holy Spirit that she has conceived. She will have a son, and you will name him Jesus- because he will save his people from their sins".*

We just have to question this!

If the angel spoke to Joseph in a dream, then how did the author of Matthew's Gospel know this? Who would have told him? Joseph? Joseph was the only living person who could possibly have known this! And bearing in mind, as Matthew tells us, that Joseph "*did not want to disgrace Mary publicly*", (Matthew1:19), then Joseph himself would hardly have broadcast it!

And, while in Matthew's Gospel, it is Joseph who is having the dream, in Luke's Gospel, it is Mary who is having the dream!

Then Matthew proceeds to tell us very specifically: "*Now all this happened in order to make what the Lord had said through the prophet come true: A virgin will become pregnant and have a son and he shall be called Immanuel (which means God is with us)".*

We just have to question this as well!

This is Matthew's first statement in his Gospel about prophecies needing to be fulfilled, a statement he continuously repeats after almost every event he describes.

This would lead us to consider was the Gospel of Matthew written around the prophecies? To fulfil them? Were the various stories made up just to fulfil the prophecies?

We shall see!

And what did the prophet Isaiah actually say about the birth of Jesus?

"Well then, the Lord himself will give you a sign, a young woman who is pregnant will have a son and will name him Immanuel". (Isaiah 7:14)

No mention of a virgin here either!

And if the child was to be called Immanuel, then why was he actually called Jesus?

And why does Matthew use the name Jesus?

And what does our second author who includes the same event, the birth of Jesus, tell us about it?

Luke writes: "*At that time the Emperor Augustus ordered a census to be taken throughout the Roman Empire. When this first census took place, Quirinius was the governor of Syria. Everyone, then, went to register himself, each to his own town. Joseph went from the town of Nazareth in Galilee to the town of Bethlehem in Judea, the birthplace of King David. Joseph went there because he was a descendant of David. He went to register with Mary who was promised in marriage to him. She was pregnant and while they were in Bethlehem, the time came for her to have her baby. She gave birth to her first son, wrapped him in strips of cloth, and laid him in a manger - there was no room for them to stay in the inn*". (Luke 2:1-7)

Certainly no mention of a virgin here!

But in the teachings of the Roman Catholic Church, the Perpetual Virginity of Mary, the mother of Jesus is paramount, non negotiable, set in concrete.

But where did this idea come from?

We may well ask!

The virgin birth story was certainly not something new when Jesus was born. Roman and Greek mythology is full of such stories, with countless tales permeating Roman religious beliefs and customs.

Ancient and early historians and writers such as Herodotus, the contemporary of Socrates in the fifth century B.C.E., Pliny the

Elder, 50 C.E., Justin Martyr, 150 C.E., Tertullian, 200 C.E., all testify to the existence and beliefs in such myths.

And where the Romans went, they took their Gods and Goddesses with them!

So now let us look at some of these myths of virgin births which spread to every part of the Roman Empire, Jewish Palestine included, taken over as part of the Roman Empire by the Roman General Pompey in 63 B.C.E.

Attis, for example, the ancient Phrygo-Roman God was believed to have been born of a virgin on December 25th. He was killed and was resurrected. His mother, Nana, also known as Cybele, was, like the Egyptian Goddess Isis, and like the Christian figure Mary, considered a perpetual virgin, despite her status as a mother.

Attis' birthday on 25th December! The same as Jesus' birthday!

What a strange coincidence!

And this despite the fact that neither Mark nor Luke give any date or time of year for the birth!

The Romans also worshipped the ancient Sun God Mithras, of the Persian-Roman religion of Mithraism, also born of a virgin. According to Persian mythology, Mithras was born on 25th December (!) son of Ormuzd and the virgin (!) Anahita, who was known as the '*Mother of God'*. The babe was born in a cave, wrapped in swaddling clothes, placed in a manger and attended by shepherds (!) It was the Emperor Constantine in 313 C.E., who declared December 25th to be the birthday of Jesus. His predecessor, Aurelian had already prescribed December 25th as the birthday of Mithras.

The Greeks also celebrated the birthday of their Sun-God Apollo on 25th December!

Mithraism had its roots in Zorastrianism, a Persian religion that became popular in Greece from about 390 B.C.E. The cult assumingly spread from Persia, reaching the west through the Roman Empire. Mithras was cast in the role of a deity equal to the Sun God. Its priests were known as 'Magi'. Zarathustra, a Zoroastrian Magi, had predicted a Messiah.

Did not the Magi come to visit the new born Jesus, the expected Messiah, bearing gifts?

Are any of those dots beginning to join?

Are any of those figures beginning to tally?

***Are any of those jig-saw pieces beginning to fit*?**

Mithras himself advocated celibacy, and his followers were celibate. They believed that after death, they would live in bliss until the final judgement of mankind, when all the dead would rise from their graves to be judged. Then Mithras would bring all his faithful followers into Paradise to live with him for all eternity, while the unbaptised and the evil would be destroyed by fire.

Does this not all seem familiar?

Anahita, Mithra's virgin mother, was also known as '*Anaitas*' which translates as '*pure*' and '*untainted*'. She was equated with the virgin Goddess Artemis, an Indo-Iranean Goddess of some antiquity, and the best known divinity of the Persians in Asia Minor.

The Egyptian Pharaohs believed that they were the Sun God Horus in human form, identifying themselves with Horus in life and with his father, Osiris in death. While Osiris ruled the dead in the underworld, Horus ruled the living. Horus too was born of a virgin, Isis who was married to Osiris.

Horus predated Jesus by 3,000 years.

'*Ra*' was the name of The Egyptian Sun God, referred to in the '*Egyptian Book of the Dead*'. One of Ra's sons and remakes was the saviour Osiris, referred to above, who, with his wife Isis, became two of the most popular Gods ever to be conceived (!) by the human mind.

So, as we can see, at the time of the birth of Jesus, there already existed a widespread devotion to numerous Gods and deities, most of whom were of virgin birth or birth by some other extraordinary means.

Certainly it is obvious that there was a curious veneration for virginity rampant throughout the Roman Empire, surviving up to the middle ages and beyond. Virgins were cast with a semi-romantic, semi-religious halo that extolled them as possessing the gifts of prophecy and ability to communicate directly with the Gods.

Let us look at some more examples!

Silvia, the wife of Septimius Marcellus, was said to have had a child by the God Mars. The mother of Romulus and Remus was also called Silvia, and was a vestal virgin named Rhea Silvia, and their father was Mars.

The Grecian God Dionysos was said to be the son of Zeus out of the virgin Goddess Persephone.

Mut-em-ua, the virgin Queen of Egypt, was said to have given birth to the Pharaoh Amenophis III who built the temple of Luxor, on the walls of which were inscribed the details of the annunciation to the virgin Queen by the God Taht that she was to be the mother of Amenophos; the conception; the birth of the man-God and the adoration of the newly born infant by Gods and men, including three kings who came bearing gifts.

And it was not just Gods who were credited with supernatural births!

Of Plato, for example, it was said that his mother Perictione was a virgin who conceived him immaculately by the God Apollo. Apollo himself revealed the circumstances of this conception to Ariston, the betrothed husband of the virgin.

Just as God sent his angel to reveal Mary' pregnancy to Joseph!

Jewish thinking did not accept the virgin birth of Jesus. The Jews did not believe in the virgin birth story because it did not have its roots in Jewish thinking. So, unlike later Christians of the Roman Catholic variety, they did not see Jesus as a Divine being.

So we can clearly see that the story of the virgin birth was nothing new at the time of the birth of Jesus. Virginity and virgin births were deeply embedded in Greco-Roman culture, evidenced by the vast amount of mythological material found in Greek and Roman Literature.

Early Christianity no doubt found itself in serious competition with other pagan cults, and of course, needed to come up with an equally miraculous, incomprehensible, incredible, but acceptable story.

And virgin births were not just acceptable, but also very desirable at that time!

It's the same old story, though, regurgitated time and time again!

Perhaps the dots are beginning to join up?

Perhaps the figures are beginning to tally?

Perhaps the jig-saw pieces are beginning to fit?

The belief that Mary's pregnancy resulted from a Divine act of God without any male involvement developed into a fundamental theological dogma in early Christianity.

But it is not in the early scriptures!

Very much history for convenience! Selective evidencing! The church using what suits, discarding what does not!

And, as we have just seen, the idea of humans being fathered by Gods was quite common in Greco-Roman culture.

Now! Here is some food for serious thought!

Ready?

In the '***Gospel of Philip***', one of the Gospels found in the desert at Nag Hammadi, in Egypt in 1945, and which did not make its way into the canonical Gospels, we read:

"*Some say that Mary was impregnated by the grace of the Holy / Spirit, but they do not know what they say. / How could the Feminine impregnate the feminine*?" (Plate 103)

And:

"The Teacher would not have said: 'My Father who is in heaven', / if he had not been engendered by another Paternity / than the one he had from his earthly father." (Plate 103)

And what exactly was found at Nag Hammadi?

A collection of thirteen ancient codices were among the findings at Nag Hammadi in 1945, many of them dating from early C.E. Included was the '***Gospel of Philip',*** the '***Gospel of Thomas***' and the '***Gospel of Mary Magdalene***', none of which found their way into the Canonical Gospels.

I wonder why?

But the virgin birth is not all we need to question about the birth of Jesus as related in the Canonical Gospels!

Time and place of Jesus' Birth

Let us now look at the date of the birth of Jesus.

Herod the Great died in 4 B.C.E.

Archelaus, Herod's son, became ruler of Judea and ruled from 4 B.C.E. until 6 C.E.

Publius Sulpicius Quirinius was a Roman aristocrat, appointed governor of Syria after Herod Archelaus was banished in 6 C.E., and Judea was added to Syria for the purpose of the census.

Archelaus was replaced by Coponius. And that was in 6 C.E.

Matthew, however, tells us: *"Jesus was born in the town of Bethlehem in Judea, during the time when Herod was king".* (Matthew 2:1)

But Herod died in 4 B.C!

According to Luke, however, Jesus was born during the first census in Israel, which was in 6 C.E., while Quirinius was governor of Syria:

"In those days, Caesar Augustus issued a decree that a census should be taken of the entire Roman world. When this first census took place, Quirinius was governor of Syria". (Luke 2:2)

But Quirinius did not become governor of Syria until well after Herod's death!

Josephus, our historian from that period, says the Quirinius census took place in 6 C.E., ten years after the death of Herod the Great!

And there is no record to be found anywhere of a census, as claimed by Luke, in the "*entire Roman world*".

Such a census would entail vast numbers of people on the move across vast territory. Yet Josephus, the Jewish historian, writing in the early first century C.E., does not mention it! Nor do any of the other early historians!

There is no record that Quirinius was governor of Syria at the time Luke specifies.

The dots just do not join up!

The figures just do not add up!

The jig-saw pieces just do not fit!

We also need to consider why Jesus was born in Bethlehem!

Maybe you now already know!

But of course! Didn't the prophecies say he would be born in Bethlehem?

So we must have Jesus born in Bethlehem! Right?

Nazareth was in the north of Judea, in Galilee. Bethlehem was in the south just outside Jerusalem, about a journey of three days away.

As we have just seen, Both Matthew and Luke say that Jesus was born in Bethlehem.

Matthew, in usual form, adds on an appendage, this time from Micah that this was in fulfillment of the prophecy*: "For this is what the prophet wrote: Bethlehem in the land of Judea..............from you will come a leader who will guide my people Israel".* (Matthew 2:6)

So the writer of the Gospel of Matthew had to have Jesus born in Bethlehem!

In order to fulfil the prophecy!

And how exactly was he going to bring this about?

As we have just seen, he very conveniently brought in the census of Quinerius, and made everyone return to his birth place to register. Register for what? Register for taxation, of course!

And what would that have had to do with where people were from? Surely it would have had more to do with where they lived and worked at present, rather than where they were from? Surely Joseph would have had to register in his taxation district rather than in his ancestral home place?

And then Matthew tries to give this some historical back-up by saying that there was no room at the inn as there were so many people there registering!

And why did Mary have to go with him? A pregnant woman about to give birth traipsing all that way to Bethlehem on a donkey?

But for what other reason were the Gospels going to get her to Bethlehem? The census, of course!

But a three day journey? In the relentless heat of the desert?

And of course, they arrive in Bethlehem just in time for Mary to give birth!

Phew! That was close! Well timed, Joseph!

Could have been a desert birth!

Well, actually no! It couldn't possibly have been a desert birth!

And why not?

Because there was no prophecy for a desert birth!

And how come, if Jesus was born in Bethlehem, he was known and referred to all his life as the '*Nazarene*'!

It looks like he was only born in Bethlehem in order to have the prophecies fulfilled!

Surprise! Surprise!

Now let us consider how both Matthew and Luke give detailed genealogies of Jesus, tracing him back through his father, Joseph, to King David.

The Genealogies of Jesus

Both Matthew and Luke include the genealogy of Jesus, but again, they are not in agreement. (Matthew 1:1-17; Luke 3:23-37)

Both go to great pains and into great detail to show how Joseph was a direct descendant from the line of David. But the great discrepancies between them give rise to serious problems in assessing authenticity.

For example, Matthew lists only 27 names between David and Jesus while Luke, on the other hand, numbers 42.

Big difference!

Matthew claims that Jesus descended from Solomon, son of David, while Luke on the other hand, claims that Jesus descended from Nathan, son of David.

Matthew claims that Joseph was the son of Jacob, while Luke claims that Joseph was the son of Heli.

But! Hold on a minute!

According to the Catholic Church, Joseph was not the biological father of Jesus!

Was Jesus not conceived of the Holy Spirit, of the virgin Mary?

So therefore, following logically on from that, and according to the thinking of the Catholic Church, Joseph had no input whatsoever into the conception of Jesus!

So why are these two authors of Matthew and Luke so determined to establish descent from the line of David?

The answer?

It's those prophecies again!

Obviously, it was necessary to establish direct descent from the line of David in order to fulfil the prophecies!

Are the dots beginning to join up?

Are the figures beginning to tally?

Are the jig-saw pieces beginning to fit?

If the Holy Spirit was the father of Jesus, then that would make it impossible to trace his line of descent back to King David!

So was Joseph just an excuse thought up in order to fulfil the prophecy?

Which prophecy this time?

"The Lord says: 'The time is coming when I will choose as king a righteous descendant of David. That king will rule wisely and do what is right and just throughout the land." (Jeremiah 22: 5)

"You made a solemn promise to David - a promise you will not take back: 'I will make one of your sons king and he will rule after you. If your sons are true to my covenant and to the commands I give them, their sons, also, will succeed you for all time as kings". (Psalms 132:11)

Again, very much a case of the Church using what is convenient for them!

Who was the father of Jesus?

As we have seen, Mark and John are the two Gospels that say nothing about the birth of Jesus. They say little or nothing about his father either.

"*But he had no sexual relations with her before she gave birth to her son*". (Matthew 1:25)

So Joseph, according to the Gospels, could not have been the father! So who was the father?

"They were all amazed. 'Where did he get all this?' they asked. 'What wisdom is this that has been given him? How does he perform miracles? Isn't he the carpenter, the son of Mary.........?" (Mark 6:2-3)

A person was never referred to in those days or recognised through reference to his mother, but through his father.

There is no reference here to Joseph being Jesus' father! And these people lived in Nazareth! A small village where everyone knew everything about everybody!

Is there a suggestion of illegitimacy here, with no mention of Jesus' father?

Matthew, of course, as usual, copies Mark.

But, Matthew Luke and John do mention Joseph.

"When Jesus finished telling these parables, he left that place and

went back to his home town. He taught in the synagogue, and those who heard him were amazed. 'Where did he get such wisdom?' they asked. 'And what about his miracles? Isn't he the carpenter's son? Isn't Mary his mother?" (Matthew 13: 53-55)

"Isn't he the son of Joseph?" (Luke 4:22)

"This man is Jesus son of Joseph, isn't he? We know his father and mother." (John 6:42)

"We have found the one whom Moses wrote about in the book of the Law and whom the prophets also wrote about. He is Jesus son of Joseph, from Nazareth". (John 8: 45)

Obviously, those surrounding Jesus did not see him as a Divine being, born of a virgin !

The notion of illegitimacy is a consistent element found in all four Gospels. Joseph was not the father of Jesus!

So who was?

Have you ever wondered what happened to Joseph after they returned from Egypt and arrived in Nazareth? Where did he disappear to? We never hear any more about him! When did he die? We never hear!

The Massacre of the Innocents

Matthew is the only Gospel that carries this story.

The murder by Herod of all the male infants! Herod who, remember, had died in 4 B.C.E!

The Jewish historian Josephus, writing in the early first century C.E., makes no mention of it!

Josephus who, like all the Jews, would have hated Herod!

Josephus, a Jewish writer, who catalogued Herod's crimes and abuses with no hesitation, many times!

So where did this story come from?

Remember the prophecy that out of Egypt would come a saviour for the Israelites?

Well, from the writer's point of view, we now have managed to have Jesus born in Bethlehem. But we need to get him ***into*** Egypt first, before we can have him coming ***out*** of Egypt again!

We need to fulfil that prophecy!

So what does Matthew do? He creates the story of Herod's murder of all the male infants, which forces Joseph and Mary to flee with the infant Jesus into Egypt! And then, when Herod dies, and is succeeded by Archelaus, what happens? Joseph and Mary return to Israel with the young Jesus!

"Then Herod, when he saw that he was deceived by the wisemen, was exceedingly angry; and he sent forth and put to death all the male children who were in Bethlehem and in all its districts, from two years old and under, according to the time which he had determined from the wise men. Then was fulfilled what was spoken by Jeremiah the prophet saying, 'A voice was heard in Ramah, lamentations, weeping and great mourning. Rachel weeping for her children, refusing to be comforted, because they are no more.'" (Matthew 2:16-18)

Prophecy fulfilled!

Or so Matthew obviously thought!

But if he had read the rest of this prophecy, he would have known it did not apply to the innocents, but to the Israelites going into exile in Babylon!

So it looks as if Matthew has been shuffling through the prophecies to see which ones he can invent a story around and make it appear to come true!

And what about Herod, who was certified dead in 4 B.C?

Herod, who claimed to be King of the Jews, appears to not have known his own scriptures! He had to ask the wise men!

Matthew: "When King Herod heard about this, (the birth of Jesus) he was very upset, and so was everyone else in Jerusalem. He called together all the chief priests and the teachers of the Law and asked them, 'Where will the Messiah be born?'

'In the town of Bethlehem in Judea', they answered. 'For this is what the prophet wrote......." (Matthew 2:3-6)

Imagine Herod not knowing that!

The dots just do not join up!

The figures just do not tally!

The jig-saw pieces just do not fit!

The Flight into Egypt

Again, Matthew is the only writer who talks about the flight into Egypt and the return to Nazareth.

Joseph went to Egypt, " *where he stayed until Herod died."* (Matthew 2:15)

But Herod the Great died in 4 B.C! It cannot be Herod Archelaus he means, because he did not die at that time, he was banished to Gaul in 6 C.E! And he was still alive when he was banished! There would have been no point whatsoever in banishing him if he were dead!

We read in Luke no mention of the flight into Egypt, only how "*a week later*", after the birth, the baby was circumcised and named Jesus.

"Then the time came for Joseph and Mary to perform the ceremony

of purification, as the law of Moses commanded. So they took the child to Jerusalem to present him to the Lord." (Luke 2:21-22)

But the Law of Moses specified that forty days after the birth was the purification time required!

"*But when Joseph heard that Archelaus had succeeded his father Herod as king of Judea, he was afraid to go there. He was given more instructions in a dream, so he went to the province of Galilee and made his home in Nazareth. And so what the prophets had said came true: 'He will be called a Nazarene' ".* (Matthew 4: 22-23)

But according to Matthew earlier, they were all in Egypt at this time!

And again*: "In this way, what the prophet Jeremiah had said came true: 'A sound is heard in Ramah, the sound of bitter weeping. Rachel is crying for her children; she refuses to be comforted, for they are dead."* (Matthew 2: 17-18)

However, as mentioned before, if Matthew had just read a few more lines of this prophecy, he would have got the right end of the stick! He even misquotes the first few lines!

"A sound is heard in Ramah, the sound of bitter weeping. Rachel is crying for her children; they are gone, and she refuses to be comforted. Stop your crying and wipe away your tears. All that you have done for your children will not go unrewarded; they will return from the enemy's land. There is hope for your future; your children will come back home. I, the Lord, have spoken". (Jeremiah 31:15)

There is no mention of children being dead in the words of Jeremiah!

Only in the words of Matthew! So Matthew has misquoted Jeremiah!

"This was done to make what the Lord had said through the prophet come true: I called my Son out of Egypt." (Matthew 2:15)

"The Lord says: 'When Israel was a child, I loved him and called him out of Egypt as my son". (Hosea 11:1)

And yet again*: "But when Joseph heard that Archelaus had succeeded his father Herod as king of Judea, he was afraid to go there. He was given more instructions in a dream, so he went to the province of Galilee and made his home in a town called Nazareth. And so what the prophets had said came true: He will be called a Nazarene".* (Matthew 2:22)

This does not say that Joseph "*returned to Nazareth*" or "*went back to Nazareth*", which was where he had been living in the first place, before he went to Bethlehem to register!

At least that's where the angel went to, according to Luke, to tell Mary the good news!

"In the sixth month of Elizabeth's pregnancy, God sent the angel Gabriel to a town in Galilee named Nazareth. He had a message for a young woman promised in marriage to a man named Joseph, who was a descendant of King David". (Luke 1:26-27)

And just for good measure, Luke reminds us that Joseph was a descendant of David!

Good plug, Luke!

The same angel told Mary that Elizabeth would also have a child*: "Remember your relative Elizabeth. It is said that she cannot have children, but she herself is now six months pregnant, even though she is very old. For there is nothing that God cannot do".* (Luke 1:36-37)

"They had no children because Elizabeth could not have any, and she and Zechariah were both very old". (Luke 1:7)

The angel must have got the directions wrong!

Was this a case of another miraculous birth? Or even a virgin birth?

And where did the idea of Elizabeth being Mary's cousin come from?

Here she is referred to by the angel as a "*relative*". Or did the angel get that wrong too?

Seems as if even the angels were confused!

What chance for us mortals then?

And just to add further confusion:

"A week later, when the time came for the baby to be circumcised, he was named Jesus, the name which the angel had given him before he had been conceived.

The time came for Joseph and Mary to perform the ceremony of purification as the Law of Moses commanded. So they took the child to Jerusalem to present him to the Lord........" (Luke 2:21-22)

But surely they were supposed to be still in Egypt?

The dots just do not join up!

The figures just do not tally!

The jig-saw pieces just do not fit!

The Siblings of Jesus

In his first letter to the Corinthians, Paul writes: "*When people criticise me this is how I defend myself: 'Haven't I the right to follow the example of the other apostles and the Lord's brothers and Peter, by taking a Christian wife with me on my travels?"* (Corinthians I, 9:4-5)

And John mentions them as well: "*Not even his brothers believed in him.*" (John 7:5)

Our main historical source is, of course Josephus, the Jewish historian. It is from Josephus that we get the first reference to the actual existence of Jesus, when Josephus writes in his '*Jewish Antiquities*' that the high priest Ananus, following the death of the Roman governor Festus, and before the new governor, Albinus arrived, unlawfully condemned to stoning for transgression of the law: "*James, the brother of Jesus, the one they call messiah*".

Indeed, because of his importance in the early Church, a letter attributed to him was included in the New Testament as the Epistle of James. But his leadership role put him in jeopardy during periods of persecution, and he was eventually put to death in Jerusalem in 62 AD.

The Gospels first mention James in Matthew 13:55: "*When Jesus finished telling these parables, he left that place and went back to his home town. He taught in the synagogue and those who heard him were amazed. 'Where did he get such wisdom?' they asked. 'And what about his miracles? Isn't he the carpenter's son? Isn't Mary his mother, and aren't James, Joseph, Simon and Judas his brothers? Aren't all his sisters living here?*" (Matthew 13:53-56)

And also in Mark 6:3, where he is listed along with three other brothers of Jesus and some un-named sisters. When Jesus went back to Nazareth and began teaching in the synagogue: "*Many people were there, and when they heard him they were all amazed. 'Where did he get all this?' they asked. 'What wisdom is this that has been given him? How does he perform miracles? Isn't this the carpenter, the son of Mary and the brother of James, Joseph, Judas and Simon? Aren't his sisters living here?*" (Mark: 6:2-3)

So according to a lot of people, Jesus had brothers!

Jesus had brothers?

Yes, Jesus had brothers!

So where did they come from?

The Catholic Church has always maintained that Jesus had no siblings!

At other times, Church apologists have tried to explain that Joseph had children from a previous marriage, and therefore they were not the actual children of Mary.

The Gospels clearly indicate otherwise!

And we know why that is! In order to bolster the doctrine of the Perpetual Virginity of Mary!

As Jesus was the first-born of Mary, his brothers therefore, must have been younger than him!

"She gave birth to her first son......." (Luke 2:7)

"Jesus was still talking to the people when his mother and brothers arrived. They stood outside asking to speak with him. So some of the people there said to him, 'Look, your mother and brothers are standing outside, and they want to speak with you". (Matthew: 12:46-47)

And after the Resurrection, when Jesus appears to some of the disciples outside the tomb, he says: *"Go and tell my brothers to go to Galilee, and there they will see me"*. (Matthew: 28:10)

Again, after the Ascension of Jesus, we read in Acts how:

"They gathered frequently to pray as a group, together with the women and with Mary the mother of Jesus and with his brothers". (Acts 1:14)

So now we know the names of Jesus' brothers!

And we have also learned that he had sisters too! At least two of them!

This gets better and better!

Luke also talks about Jesus' brothers*: "Jesus' mother and brothers came to him, but were unable to join him because of the crowd".* (Luke 8:19)

And John: *"After this, Jesus and his mother, brothers and disciples went to Capernaum and stayed there a few days".* (John 2: 12)

And it was James, the brother of Jesus, who succeeded Jesus in his ministry. James, his brother, who succeeded him in the kingly line of David.

Not Peter! Peter whom we have been led to believe by the Catholic Church was the first pope and successor of Jesus!

And why has the church insisted on establishing and perpetuating Peter as the successor to Jesus, and not his brother James?

It's that perpetual virginity theory again! If Jesus is seen to have a brother, then that theory is dead in the water!

And a lot of egg on a lot of faces!

So James has to be kept under wraps! Labelled '*Not for public consumption*'!

So where then, did all these siblings come from?

How do we find that out?

"That same day some Sadducees came to Jesus and *claimed the people will not rise from death. 'Teacher', they said, 'Moses said that if a man who has no children dies, his brother must marry the widow so that they can have children who will be considered the dead man's children.'* (Matthew 22: 23-24)

"If two brothers live on the same property and one of them dies, leaving no son, then his widow is not to be married to someone outside the family; it is the duty of the dead man's brother to marry her. The first son that they have will be considered the son of the dead man, so that his family line will continue in Israel. But if the dead man's brother does not want to marry her, she is to go before the town leaders and say, 'My husband's brother will not do his duty; he refuses to give his brother a descendant among the people of Israel.' Then the town leaders are to summon him and speak to him. If he still refuses to marry her, his brother's widow is to go up to him in the presence of the town leaders, take off one of his sandals, spit in his face, and say, 'This is what happens to the man who refuses to give his brother a descendant'. His family will be known in Israel as the family of the man who had his sandal pulled off". (Deuteronomy: 25:5-10)

So did Joseph's younger brother marry Mary after Joseph died?

When did Joseph die anyway? We hear nothing more about him after the return from Egypt! He does not even die! He just disappears!

Tradition has it that Joseph was a lot older than Mary, so he probably died when Jesus was young, but why are we not told about this?

Obviously, again, to divert us from the truth that Mary remarried, and had further children! That would mean exit '*blessed Mary ever virgin*'! End of!

On the other hand, we read in Leviticus:

"*If a man marries his brother's wife, they will die childless. He has done a ritually unclean thing and has disgraced his brother*". (Leviticus: 20:21)

See how the prophecies can contradict each other?

It was this same piece of scripture that was resurrected (!) during the time of Henry VIII, 1509-1533, in order to force the then pope, Clement VII to grant an annulment to Henry from his marriage to Catherine of Aragon, his first wife.

Catherine was the widow of Henry's older brother Arthur who had died from drowning. Henry was given a special dispensation from the Church to marry Catherine, as such a marriage between a man and his dead brother's widow was forbidden.

When Henry became infatuated with Anne Boleyn, Henry's chief Church men were sent scrambling for a reason to justify an annulment from Catherine.

Cardinal Wolsey, the wealthiest man in England, and, as Lord Chancellor the most powerful only after Henry himself, failed to secure the annulment and was stripped of office. He was summoned to London to give an account of himself, but mercifully for him, he died on the way. It was his successor, Archbishop Cranmer, who unearthed the words of Leviticus, and argued that the pope should never have granted the special dispensation allowing Henry to marry Catherine, because, as a result, the marriage was cursed.

Not exactly childless, however!

A daughter emerged, the future Queen Mary Tudor, but it was a son Henry wanted. A strong son who would succeed him, perpetuate the Tudor dynasty and maintain England as a powerful country.

The people of England did not have much liking for the pope at this time. Yes, he was head of the Catholic Church, but more relevant to their lives was the fact that he was a remote foreigner who was only interested in raising taxes from them.

So, we can see that the scriptures were used to the advantage of whoever wanted to make a point or score a victory. Manipulation for a particular means and a particular end!

Just like the authors of the four Canonical Gospels!

Further evidence for the importance of his role is found in the Gospel of Thomas. The Gospel of Thomas was one of the Gospels found in Egypt, hidden in the desert, near Nag Hammadi in 1945. According to Saying 12 of this Gospel, the disciples said to Jesus:

" 'We are aware that you will depart from us. Who will be our leader?'

Jesus answered: 'No matter where you come from, it is to James the Just that you shall go, for whose sake heaven and earth have come to exist.' "

This passage clearly indicates that Jesus designated James to take over the leadership of his ministry after his death.

I wonder why this Gospel of Thomas did not find its way into the Canonical Gospels?

Some Christians think that James was actually a step-brother of Jesus, or possibly only a cousin, because they believe that Mary remained a virgin throughout her life and therefore couldn't have given birth to any children except Jesus. But Matthew, Mark, Paul, together with the early historians Josephus and Hegesippus all appear to say that James was a full brother, and most modern scholars have reached the same conclusion.

The Missing Years

Have you ever thought it very strange that we know nothing about Jesus from he was twelve years of age, teaching in the temple and astounding people with his words, until he is thirty years old and beginning his ministry?

Where was he all that time?

And even more strange! How come those same authors of the Gospels who can tell us in great detail what the angel said to Mary, what was said by the angel to Joseph in a dream, and what was said by the devil to Jesus in the desert when there was no one else there, can not tell us anything about where Jesus was in what we call the '*missing years*'?

Was Jesus married?

We certainly cannot have that! A married Jesus?

There goes the celibacy ideal of the Catholic Church!

Was he living in Nazareth? Was he a carpenter? Was he helping to support his younger brothers and sisters?

Did his mother re-marry?

We cannot have that either!

There goes the Perpetual Virginity of Mary! Again!

If Joseph had died, and Joseph's brother had married Mary and they had a family, then Jesus would surely have been helping to maintain them.

But as a carpenter, living in a tiny, poor village such as Nazareth, there would have been little or no work for him!

So where was he?

We have the cosy image presented to us by the Church that Jesus was a carpenter, living with his mother and father in Nazareth, working with his father in the family business.

Jesus was a devout Jew, living in Judea in the first years of the first century C.E!

So, having firmly established this historical truth, let us delve deeper into what life was like for such a person as Jesus, living in that particular place and at that particular time!

A Jewish father had five responsibilities towards his male offspring, responsibilities and commitments which all Jews took very seriously.

Firstly, he had to have his newly-born son circumcised at the temple just eight days after he was born.

Secondly, the parents of the child had to bring a sin offering to the temple. Wealthy parents would have brought a calf, sheep or goat, while poorer parents would have brought two doves. Joseph and Mary brought two doves:

"*The time came for Joseph and Mary to perform the ceremony of purification, as the Law of Moses commanded. So they took the child to Jerusalem to present him to the Lord, as it is written in the law of the Lord: 'Every firstborn male is to be dedicated to the Lord'. They also went to offer a sacrifice of a pair of doves or two young pigeons, as required by the law of the Lord*". (Luke 2:22:24)

Thirdly, a Jewish father had to teach his son the Torah. The word Torah, as we have seen, was the Hebrew word for law, meaning direction, guidance and instruction, and included the books of Genesis, Exodus, Leviticus, Numbers and Deuteronomy.

Fourthly, he had to teach his son a trade, so that when his son became an adult, he would in turn be able to support his own family.

And fifthly, it was a Jewish father's responsibility to find a wife for his son before he was twenty years of age.

Jews took the latter very seriously indeed!

In the book of Genesis it was written: "*He created them male and female, blessed them and said: 'Have many children so that your descendants will live all over the earth and bring it under their control.'* " (Genesis 1: 28)

And again: "*It is not good for the man to live alone*". (Genesis 2:18)

If a Jewish male reached twenty or beyond without being married, he would certainly have been commented upon by the rest of his society, and his celibate state would have been a cause for much discussion and speculation, especially by those who may have been his enemies, and they would most certainly have used this against him.

So, was Jesus married?

His apostles were!

So what about those missing years?

The Apostles of Jesus

We have always been led to believe that Jesus had twelve apostles, all male!

What were their names?

Well, according to Matthew: *"These are the names of the twelve apostles: first, Simon, (called Peter) , and his brother Andrew; James and his brother John the sons of Zebedee; Philip and Bartholomew; Thomas and Matthew the tax collector; James son of Alphaeus, and Thaddaeus; Simon the Patriot, and Judas Iscariot, who betrayed Jesus."* (Matthew 10:2-4)

Yet according to Luke: "*When day came, he called his disciples to him, and chose twelve of them, whom he named apostles: Simon, (whom he named Peter), and his brother Andrew, James and John, Philip and Bartholomew, Matthew and Thomas, James son of Alphaeus, and Simon (who was called the Patriot) and Judas son of James, and Judas Iscariot, who became the traitor."* (Luke 6:12-16)

So Luke maintains that two of Jesus' disciples went by the name of Judas, whereas Matthew has only one Judas in the group!

Jesus recruited his disciples from the community in which he grew up, at least four of them being fishermen.

"The members of the Council were amazed to see how bold Peter and John were and to learn that they were ordinary men of no education." (Acts: 4:13)

Certainly not the sort of men who would be able to write the

Gospels!

We learned earlier on that Jesus' brothers were called James, Joseph, Judas and Simon.

So were Jesus' brothers amongst his disciples?

We are diverted from finding this out because, remember! Mary's Perpetual Virginity is at stake here! Jesus just cannot be seen to have any brothers!

Now we learn that also in the group was a tax collector, Matthew, and a Patriot, Simon!

"*Simon, who was called the Patriot*" (Luke 6:15)

"*Simon the Patriot*" (Acts 1:13)

The tax collectors, whom everyone hated!

And would having a tax collector and a Patriot in the same group have led to good group dynamics?

I don't think so!

More like group dynamite!

Tax collectors were very much in league with Rome and there were probably no two groups of Jews in Palestine who hated each other more than the tax collectors and the Patriots, also called the '*Zealots*', because of their intense '*Zeal* ' in opposing Roman rule.

These Zealots had despised Herod for all that he represented. He was a Roman king, not a Jewish king and had become ruler of the Jews only through Roman help, boasting that he was '*the emperor's friend*'.

Then there were the '*Sacarii*', or dagger men, named after their '*sicae'*, their sharp curved knives which they carried discretely hidden beneath the folds of their garments. The Sicarii carried out swift assassinations, disappearing quickly back into the crowd again. They were always on the alert and ready to seize any opportune moment to assassinate any Roman official or supporter.

Did Jesus have one of these in his midst?

"*But now," Jesus said, 'whoever has a purse or a bag must take it, and whoever has no sword must sell his coat and buy one. For I tell you that the scripture which says 'He shared the fate of criminals', must come true about me, because what was written about me is coming true.'*

The disciples said, 'Look! Here are two swords, Lord!

'That is enough!' he replied." (Luke 22: 36-38)

"When the disciples who were with Jesus saw what was going to happen, they asked, 'Shall we use our swords, Lord?' And one of them struck the High Priest's slave, and cut off his right ear." (Luke 22:49-50)

"Simon Peter, who had a sword, drew it and struck the High Priest's slave, cutting off his right ear. The name of the slave was Malchus. Jesus said to Peter, 'Put your sword back in its place! Do you think that I will not drink the cup of suffering which my Father has given

me?" (John 18:10-11)

"*One of those who were with Jesus drew his sword and struck at the High Priest's slave, cutting off his ear".* (Matthew 26:51)

Such a crime obviously went unpunished, according to the gospels, as there is no mention of any arrest or punishment being meted out for Peter.

A motley crew, indeed, one might say!

Then of course, we have Judas!

"*Judas went straight to Jesus and said, 'Peace be with you, Teacher', and kissed him.*

Jesus answered, 'Be quick about it, friend!'

Then they came up, arrested Jesus and held him tight. One of those who were with Jesus drew his sword and struck at the High Priest's slave, cutting off his ear. 'Put your sword back in its place', Jesus said to him. 'All who take the sword will die by the sword. Don't you know that I could call on my Father for help, and at once he would send me more than twelve armies of angels? But in that case, how could the Scriptures come true which say that this is what must happen?............But all this has happened in order to make what the prophets wrote in the Scriptures come true'.

Then all the disciples left him and ran away." (Matthew 26:49-56)

Thanks to John, we now know who it was who cut off the ear!

"*Simon Peter, who had a sword, drew it and struck the High Priest's slave, cutting off his right ear."* (John 18:10)

Simon Peter!

A wise choice by Jesus?

Now we must ask the question, if Jesus was preaching peace, what was Peter doing carrying a sword?

And Peter was not the only one carrying a sword!

"Shall we use our swords Lord?" (Luke 22:50

Certainly a lot of violent tempers!

Not only the tax collector and the Patriot, but add to that Peter's volatility, and there is a real simmering cauldron!

Now here is an interesting point!

"Then Peter spoke up. 'Look', he said, 'we have left everything and followed you. What shall we have?'

Jesus said to them, 'You can be sure that when the Son of Man sits on his glorious throne in the New Age, then you twelve followers of mine will also sit on thrones, to rule the twelve tribes of Israel". (Matthew 19:27-28)

Luke carries the same incident: "*Then Peter said, "Look, we have left our homes to follow you".* (Luke: 18:28)

James and John wanted to be Jesus' deputies!

Mark: "*Then James and John, the sons of Zebedee, came to Jesus. 'Teacher,' they said, 'there is something we want you to do for us.'*

'What is it?' Jesus asked them.

When you sit on your throne in your glorious Kingdom, we want you to let us sit with you, one at your right and one at your left'...........When the other ten disciples heard about it, they became angry with James and John". (Mark 11:35-41)

So the disciples were looking for rewards!

Ambitious!

According to Acts, Jesus' twelve disciples were instrumental in spreading his teachings and the Christian religion after his death.

Yes, they may well have spread the teachings of Jesus after his death, but they certainly did not spread Christianity!

And why not?

Because Jesus was not a Christian!

Jesus was a Jew!

Jesus was a human being, a man, made of flesh and blood, like all humans. Not a deified man! A real flesh and blood man!

And his disciples did not see Jesus as a deity!

Jesus' early followers saw him as the Messiah, a human King of the House of David, who was going to save Israel from Roman rule.

As we have seen, it was Paul who deified and mythologised Jesus!

And it was Paul who saw Jesus as a sacrificial figure!

Peter's Mother-in-law

We have always been led to believe that Peter and the disciples were not married. Right?

But! We are specifically told in Matthew's Gospel that Jesus went to visit the house of Peter's mother-in-law!

"Jesus went to Peter's home, and there he saw Peter's mother-in-law sick in bed with a fever". (Matthew 8:14)

Mark: *"Jesus and his disciples, including James and John, left the synagogue and went straight to the home of Simon and Andrew. Simon's mother-in-law was sick in bed with a fever"* (Mark: 1:29-30)

Luke: *"So Jesus left the synagogue and went to Simon's house. Simon's mother-in-law was sick with a high fever."* (Luke 4:38)

Now, there is only one way in which one can acquire a mother-in-law! And that is to be married! Right?

The dots just don't join up!

The figures just do not tally!

The jig-saw pieces just do not fit!

Furthermore, in his first letter to the Corinthians, Paul writes: "*When people criticise me this is how I defend myself: 'Haven't I the right to follow the example of the other apostles and the Lord's brothers and Peter, by taking a Christian wife with me on my travels?*" (Corinthians One: 9:4-5)

So, according to Paul, the apostles were married!

So why does the Catholic Church attempt to hide all this?

It's that celibacy thing again! That Church obsession!

Where, one might well ask, do those who propagate this celibacy idea, along with the virgin birth, think we all come from? And where do they think they themselves have come from?

Surely not more virgin births!

The Anointing of Jesus by Mary Magdalene

Mary Magdalene has been given a very unfair press in the Gospels. Branded and castigated as a prostitute, a sinner and even as one possessed by devils, her image has been totally distorted for reasons which are only now becoming obvious.

As has been shown clearly in other Gospels, those which the Catholic Church did not include in the canonical four, Mary Magdalene is an equal of Jesus, far superior in understanding of his words than were any of the other apostles.

And how do the Canonical Gospels portray her?

Why do these Gospels degrade her?

Again, the answer lies in the fact that from the point of view of the Church, any sort of contact Jesus has with any woman other than his virgin mother, would negate his perfection of divinity!

But the doctrine of the Council of Chalcedon proclaimed:

"Christ is at once perfect (totus) in his divinity and perfect (totus) in his humanity."

There is quite clearly a blatant contradiction in all of this! Right?

The Council of Chalcedon was the fourth ecumenical Council of the Christian Church, held from October 8th to November 1st in 451 C.E. Its main edit was '*The Chalcedonian Definition*', an attempt to settle the dispute about the divinity of Jesus. Not all Christians agreed with this teaching. Chalcedon was then the city of Bithynia in Asia Minor, on the Asian side of the Bosphorus, now in modern times part of the Istanbul Province of Turkey.

In the Canonical Gospels, Mary Magdalene is the woman who anoints Jesus with the expensive oil.

All four Gospels carry the story of the anointing of Jesus by the woman with the alabaster jar, but as usual, we get different versions.

Mark places the incident in Bethany, in the house of Simon, and has Mary anointing Jesus' head:

"Jesus was in Bethany at the house of Simon, a man who had suffered from a dreaded skin disease. While Jesus was eating, a woman came in with an alabaster jar full of a very expensive perfume made of pure nard. She broke the jar and poured the perfume on Jesus' head. Some of the people there became angry and said to one another, 'What was the use of wasting the perfume? It could have been sold for more than three hundred silver coins and the money given to the poor!' And they criticised her harshly.

But Jesus said, 'Leave her alone! Why are you bothering her? She has done a fine and beautiful thing for me. You will always have poor people with you, and any time you want to, you can help them. But you will not always have me. She did what she could; she poured perfume on my body to prepare it ahead of time for burial. Now, I assure you that wherever the gospel is preached all over the world, what she has done will be told in memory of her". (Mark 14:3-9)

Matthew, as usual, repeats Mark almost word for word (Matthew 26:6-13)

Luke changes the story, making it seem a completely different incident, not naming the woman, only referring to her as a sinner, and having her anoint Jesus' feet:

"A pharisee invited Jesus to have dinner with him, and Jesus went to his house and sat down to eat. In that town was a woman who lived a sinful life. She heard that Jesus was eating in the Pharisee's house, so she brought al alabaster jar full of perfume and stood behind Jesus by his feet, crying and wetting his feet with her tears. Then she dried his feet with her hair, kissed them, and poured the

perfume on them. When the Pharisee saw this, he said to himself, 'If this man really were a prophet, he would know who this woman is who is touching him; he would know what kind of sinful life she lives!'

Jesus spoke up and said to him, 'Simon, I have something to tell you.........Do you see this woman? I came into your house, and you gave me no water for my feet, but she has washed my feet with her tears and dried them with her hair. You did not welcome me with a kiss, but she has not stopped kissing my feet since I came. You provided no oil for my head, but she has covered my feet with perfume. I tell you, then, the great love she has shown proves that her many sins have been forgiven. But whoever has been forgiven little shows only a little love'.

Then Jesus said to the woman 'Your sins are forgiven.' " (Luke 7:36-48)

So if the Pharisee said things to himself, then how does Luke know to repeat it?

John places the same event in Holy Week, in the home of Lazarus, but before, rather than after Jesus' triumphant entry into Jerusalem:

"Six days before the Passover, Jesus went to Bethany, the home of Lazarus, the man he had raised from death. They prepared a dinner for him there, which Martha helped to serve; Lazarus was one of those who were sitting at the table with Jesus. Then Mary took half a litre of a very expensive perfume made of pure nard, poured it on Jesus' feet, and wiped them with her hair. The sweet smell of the perfume filled the whole house. One of Jesus' disciples, Judas

Iscariot - the one who was going to betray him - - said, 'Why wasn't this perfume sold for three hundred silver coins and the money given to the poor?' He said this, not because he cared about the poor, but because he was a thief. He carried the money bag and would help himself from it.

But Jesus said, 'Leave her alone. Let her keep what she has for the day of my burial. You will always have poor people with you, but you will not always have me". (John 12:1-8)

So John is calling Judas a thief! The money bag was the communal purse for the apostles as they travelled together from place to place, and John is saying that Judas was helping himself!

Interesting!

The Ministry of Jesus

Jesus constantly refers to himself throughout his ministry as '*Son of Man*' and not '*Son of God*'. (Mark 10:23; Matthew 16:27; Matthew 17:9; Luke 20:27; Luke 22:22)

Surely this must mean that he did not see himself in any way as a divine being, but a son of mortal man!

And he repeatedly told his disciples not to announce him as the Messiah!

"Do not tell any one about me!" (Mark 8:27)

Why not?

Surely he wanted people to know that he was the Messiah?

And what was he doing preaching to huge crowds if he did not want anyone to know about him?

The dots just do not join up!

The figures just do not tally!

The jig-saw pieces just do not fit!

How else did he see himself?

"*Do not think that I have come to bring peace to the world. No, I did not come to bring peace, but a sword. I came to set sons against their fathers, daughters against their mothers, daughters-in-law against their mothers-in-law; your worst enemies will be the members of your own family".* (Matthew 10: 34-46)

Why do the Gospels portray Jesus in this manner?

Where is the peace loving Jesus here?

Admittedly, Jesus was certainly surrounded by hotheads! Peter and others were carrying knives, and Peter cut off the servant's ear. And as we saw, Jesus had Simon the Patriot in his group!

And why do the Gospels portray Jesus as always being at odds with the Pharisees?

Jesus himself was a Pharisee!

First, let us consider the Pharisees, probably the best known Jewish sect, from our reading of the Gospels.

Josephus tells us: "*Now the Pharisees simplify their way of life and give in to no sort of softness; and they follow the guidance of what their doctrine has handed down and prescribes as good; and they earnestly strive to observe the commandments it dictates to them. They also show respect to the elders, nor are they so bold as to contradict them in any thing they have introduced. Although they determine that all things are done by fate, they do not take away the freedom from men as acting as they think fit; since it has pleased God to make a combination of his council-chamber and of the people who wish to approach with their virtue and their vice. They also believe that souls have an immortal power in them, and that under the earth there will be rewards or punishments according to whether they showed virtue or vice in this life; the latter are to be detained in an everlasting prison, but the former are allowed an easy passage through and live again. Because of these doctrines they hold great influence among the populace, and all divine worship, prayers, and sacrifices are performed according to their direction. In doing so the cities bear witness to their virtuous conduct, both in their way of life and in their words.*" (*'Antiquities'* 18.1.2-3)

However, in the Gospel of Matthew we see a different view of the Pharisees when we read how Jesus spoke to the crowds and to his disciples: "*The teachers of the Law and the Pharisees are the authorized interpreters of Moses' Law. So you must obey and follow everything they tell you to do; do not, however, imitate their actions, because they don't practise what they preach.......they do everything so that people will see them.........they love the best places at feasts and the reserved seats in the synagogues. They love to be greeted with respect and to be called Teacher."* (Matthew 23:2-7)

Addressing the Pharisees themselves, Jesus calls them: "*You hypocrites! ....Blind guides!....... Blind fools!..........You clean the outside of your cup and plate, while the inside is full of what you have obtained by violence and selfishness..........you are like whitewashed tombs.... on the outside you appear good to everybody, but inside you are full of hypocrisy and sins."* (Matthew 23: 13-28)

This is how most Christians tend to see the Pharisees,- as hypocrites!

Luke furthers this impression: "*How terrible for you teachers of the Law! You have kept the key that opens the door to the house of knowledge; you yourselves will not go in, and you stop those who are trying to go in!"* (Luke 11:52)

As does Mark: "*A large crowd was listening to Jesus gladly. As he taught them, he said, 'Watch out for the teachers of the Law, who like to walk around in their long robes, and be greeted with respect in the market place, who choose the reserved seats in the synagogues and the best places at feasts. They take advantage of widows and rob them of their homes, and then make a show of saying long prayers. Their punishment will be all the worse!"* (Mark 12:38-40)

What Josephus and Matthew do agree upon, however, is the dependence the people had on the Pharisees to instruct them in doctrine.

Whatever way we see them though, the Pharisees were a highly religious group who emphasised the importance of keeping the Law given to them by God. They were members of Jewish middle class families who were committed to upholding the Law of Moses. That Law however, was very vague and unclear in the instructions as to how exactly one should obey the Law, and so this gave rise to lots of arguments, questioning, debate and discussion, for which the Pharisees were noted, all aimed at identifying the best way for people to keep the Law.

We see throughout the Gospels how Jesus was constantly in conflict with the Pharisees over their intent and over-concern about keeping the Law, for example in observing the Law of rest on the Sabbath, but disagreements and conflict were part of everyday life amongst all the different and various sects in Judaism.

So if the Pharisees were indeed an enlightened, progressive sect, as has been depicted by the historian Josephus, then why do the Gospels have Jesus criticize them so harshly?

And why do the Gospels depict such antagonism on both sides?

The whole depiction of Jesus constantly at loggerheads with the Pharisees is obviously one of the many examples of early Christian Church re-editing!

In the first written Gospel, Mark, Jesus is interacting with the '*Lawyer*' or the Pharisee in a friendly, discussive exchange, which as we have seen, was typical of the Pharisee agenda. The Pharisee admires Jesus for his reply:

"A teacher of the Law was there who heard the discussion. He saw that Jesus had given the Sadducees a good answer, so he came to him with a question: 'Which commandment is the most important of all?'

Jesus replied, 'The most important one is this: 'Listen, Israel! The Lord your God is the only Lord. Love the Lord your God with all your heart, with all your soul, with all your mind, and with all your strength.' The second most important commandment is this: 'Love your neighbor as you love yourself.' There is no other commandment more important that these two.'

The teacher of the Law said to Jesus, 'Well done, Teacher! It is true, as you say, that only the Lord is God and that there is no other god but he. And to love with all your heart and with all your mind and with all your strength, and to love your neighbour as yourself, is more important than to offer animals and other sacrifices to God.'

Jesus noticed how wise his answer was, and so he told him, 'You are not far from the Kingdom of God." (Mark 12:28-34)

Here we are seeing a friendly exchange between Jesus and the Pharisee, with a strong tone of agreeableness and admiration.

Then Matthew, who usually copies Mark, surprises us with a completely different tone to the same exchange!

"One of them , a Teacher of the Law, tried to trap him with a question. 'Teacher', he asked 'which is the greatest commandment in the Law?'

Jesus answered, 'Love the Lord with all your heart, with all your soul and with all your mind. This is the greatest and the most important commandment. The second most important commandment is like it: Love your neighbour as you love yourself. The whole Law of Moses and the teachings of the prophets depend on these two commandments'. " (Matthew 22:34-40)

In Matthew, the friendliness of the exchange has been substituted with an attempt simply to test Jesus, to trap him, to catch him out.

So what exactly is going on here?

We may well ask!

Apparently a process of editing is going on in to make some sort of disagreement obvious!

Another example of disagreement between Jesus and the Pharisees is the question of Jesus healing on the Sabbath:

In Luke's Gospel, we read: "*One Sabbath Jesus went to eat a meal at the home of one of the leading Pharisees; and people were watching Jesus closely. A man whose legs and arms were swollen came to Jesus, and Jesus asked the teachers of the Law and the Pharisees , 'Does our Law allow healing on the Sabbath or not?'*

But they would not say anything. Jesus took the man, healed him, and then sent him away. Then he said to them, 'If any one of you had a son or an ox that happened to fall into a well on a Sabbath, would you not pull them out at once on the Sabbath itself?'

But they were not able to answer him about this." (Luke 14:1-6)

"Some people were there who wanted to accuse Jesus of doing wrong; so they watched him closely to see whether he would heal the man on the Sabbath. Jesus said to the man, 'Come up here to the front'. Then he asked the people, 'What does our Law allow us to do on the Sabbath? To help or to harm? To save someone's life or to destroy it?'

But they did not say a thing. Jesus was angry as he looked round at them, but at the same time he felt sorry for them, because they were so stubborn and wrong. Then he said to the man, 'Stretch out your hand.' He stretched out his hand and it became well again. So the Pharisees left the synagogue and met at once with some members of Herod's party, and they made plans to kill Jesus." (Mark 3:2-6)

So not only do these Pharisees criticise Jesus for healing on the Sabbath, but they plot to kill him for the same reason!

So what could have been the motive for portraying Jesus as being in conflict with the Pharisees, of whom he himself was one?

The Pharisees were the keepers, the custodians, the chief authorities of Judaic religious laws.

And it was of the utmost importance to the Gospel writers to make Jesus appear to be in conflict with these authorities.

And why was this so important?

This was so important because no charge could be found against Jesus on political grounds. He was not causing any political or civil unrest, and so no political charge could be brought against him.

The charges just had to be religious!

The Pharisees were, in reality, not in any way antagonistic towards or in disagreement with Jesus. This is obvious when some of them actually warned Jesus about the danger from Herod:

"At that same time some Pharisees came to Jesus and said to him, 'You must get out of here and go somewhere else, because Herod wants to kill you'." (Luke 13:31)

Now, we must ask ourselves, why should these Pharisees who, just a short while ago, were trying to plot Jesus' death for healing on the Sabbath, now want to save him?

Once again!

The dots just do not join up!

The figures just do not tally!

The jig-saw pieces just do not fit!

The only sensible conclusion that we can come to is that the stories about conflict between Jesus and the Pharisees were fabricated!

Or they were re-edited!

Why?

Obviously to show Jesus as being a rebel against Jewish religion!

As we shall see later, in the trial and sentencing of Jesus, it was the

Jewish crowd who demanded Jesus' Crucifixion!

That same crowd who had welcomed him with shouts of joy and jubilation as he entered Jerusalem just a few days before!

The Jews were framed!

As was Jesus!

The Jews were framed to demand the death of Jesus, who in turn had been made to appear to be in opposition to the teachings of the Jewish religion!

Propaganda! Spin! Manipulation! Re-editing!

It's all there in the Gospels!

John the Baptiser

"This is the Good News about Jesus Christ, the Son of God. It began as the prophet Isaiah had written. 'God said, 'I will send my messenger ahead of you to clear the way for you. Someone is shouting in the desert, 'Get the road ready for the Lord; make a straight path for him to travel.'

So John appeared in the desert, baptizing and preaching. 'Turn away from your sins and be baptized', he told the people, 'and God will forgive your sins'. Many people from the province of Judea and the city of Jerusalem went out to hear John. They confessed their sins, and he baptized them in the River Jordan.

John wore clothes made of camel's hair, with a leather belt round his waist, and his food was locusts and wild honey. He announced to the people, 'The man who will come after me is much greater than I am. I am not good enough even to bend down and untie his sandals. I baptize you with water, but he will baptize you with the Holy Spirit." (Mark1:1-8)

"At that time John the Baptist came to the desert of Judea and started preaching. 'Turn away from your sins', he said, 'because the Kingdom of heaven is near'. John was the man the prophet Isaiah was talking about when he said: 'Someone is shouting in the desert, 'Prepare a road for the Lord; make a straight path for him to travel.'

John's clothes were made of camel's hair; he wore a leather belt round his waist, and his food was locusts and wild honey. People came to him from Jerusalem from the whole province of Judea, and from all the country near the River Jordan. They confessed their sins, and he baptized them in the Jordan." (Matthew 3: 1-6)

"I baptize you with water to show that you have repented, but the one who will come after me will baptize you with the Holy Spirit and fire. He is much greater than I am; and I am not good enough even to carry his sandals." (Matthew 3:11)

So here we are, being told by John himself that he baptized for repentance. Is that not what he has just said?

But! If Jesus was sinless, as we have always been led to believe, and free from original sin, then he would have nothing to repent. So why then did he need to be baptized by anybody, never mind by John the Baptizer?

Or could it be that, just perhaps, just maybe, Jesus was not sinless?

"Why do you call me good?' Jesus asked him. 'No one is good except God alone'. (Mark 10:18)

Repeated by Matthew of course!

"Why do you ask me concerning what is good?' answered Jesus. 'There is only One who is good". (Matthew 19:17)

Repeated by Luke: *"Why do you call me good?' Jesus asked him. 'No one is good except God alone'.* (Luke 18: 19)

There also seems to be a discrepancy in Luke's Gospel as to when Jesus was baptized, as Luke has him baptized after John is imprisoned!

"Until the time of John, all the prophets and the Law of Moses spoke about the Kingdom; and if you are willing to believe their message, John is Elijah, whose coming was predicted. Listen then if you have ears!" (Matthew 11:14)

"At that time Jesus arrived from Galilee and came to John at the Jordan to be baptized by him. But John tried to make him change his mind. 'I ought to be baptized by you,' John said, 'and yet you have come to me!'

But Jesus answered him, 'Let it be so for now. For in this way we shall do all that God requires'. So John agreed." (Matthew 3:13-15)

Again, fulfilling the prophecy!

"John spoke about him. He cried out, 'This is the one I was talking

about, when I said, 'He comes after me, but he is greater than I am, because he existed before I was born.' (John 1:15)

So John recognised Jesus as the Messiah!

"Then tell us who you are,' they said. 'We have to take an answer back to those who sent us. What do you say about yourself?'

John answered by quoting the prophet Isaiah: 'I am the voice of someone shouting in the desert: 'Make a straight path for the Lord to travel!'

The messengers, who had been sent by the Pharisees, then asked John, 'If you are not the Messiah nor Elijah nor the Prophet, why do you baptize?'

John answered, 'I baptize with water, but among you stands the one you do not know. He is coming after me, but I am not good enough even to untie his sandals.'

All this happened in Bethany on the east side of the River Jordan, where John was baptizing." (John 1:22-28)

How come these are all adults being baptized?

How come no children were getting baptized?

And for what would a baby have to repent?

The first encounter, contrary to common belief, between Jesus and John the Baptiser was not at the Baptism of Jesus.

It was thirty years earlier, in fact, when they both recognised and acknowledged each other from their respective wombs!

"For as soon as I heard your greeting, the babe within me jumped with gladness." (Luke 1: 44)

Years later, when John is baptising, he refers to Jesus as the "*Lamb of God who takes away the sins of the world",* and the "*Son of God*" (John 1:29-36

John certainly seems to have known Jesus and accepted him as the Messiah!

Yet, when he is in prison he does not know if Jesus is the Messiah!

"When John's disciples told him about all these things, he called two of them and sent them to the Lord to ask him, 'Are you the one John said was going to come, or if we should expect someone else". (Luke 7:20)

"When John the Baptist heard in prison about the things that Christ was doing, he sent some of his disciples to him. 'Tell us', they asked Jesus, 'are you the one John said was going to come, or should we expect someone else?" (Matthew 11:2-3)

A very confused John the Baptist!

And what did Jesus think of John?

"Tell me, what did you go out to see? A prophet? Yes indeed, but you saw much more than a prophet. For John is the one of whom the scripture says: 'God said, I will send my messenger ahead of you to open the way for you'. I assure you that John the Baptist is

greater than anyone who has ever lived. But the one who is least in the Kingdom of heaven is greater than John." (Matthew 11:9-11)

We must ask ourselves, of course the obvious question, that if John knew that Jesus was the expected Messiah, then why did he and his followers not join Jesus and become the disciples of Jesus?

And what are we told about John's death?

"It was on Herod's birthday, when he gave a great feast for all the chief government officials, the military commanders, and the leading citizens of Galilee. The daughter of Herodias came in and danced, and pleased Herod and his guests. So the king said to the girl, 'What would you like to have? I will give you anything you want.' With many vows he said to her, 'I swear that I will give you anything you ask for, even as much as half my kingdom!'

So the girl went out and asked her mother, 'What shall I ask for?'

'The head of John the Baptist,' she answered.

The girl hurried back at once to the king and demanded. 'I want you to give me here and now the head of John the Baptist on a dish!'

This made the king very sad, but he could not refuse her because of the vow he had made in front of all his guests. So he sent off a guard at once with orders to cut John's head off, then he brought it on a dish and gave it to the girl who gave it to her mother." (Mark 6: 21-28)

Matthew repeats, from Mark (Matthew 14:1-12)

Luke, however, this time, contrary to expectations, does not embellish the tale! In fact, he plays the whole incident down!

"When Herod, the ruler of Galilee, heard about all the things that were happening, he was very confused, because some people were saying that John the Baptist had come back to life. Others were saying that Elijah had appeared, and still others that one of the prophets of long ago had come back to life. Herod said, 'I had John's head cut off; but who is this man I hear these things about?' And he kept trying to see Jesus." (Luke 9: 7-9)

So we have Mark elaborating the tale, then Matthew copying Mark's version, and Luke giving us nothing at all about the death of John the Baptist!

So we are still left wondering, how did John the Baptist die?

The Transfiguration

A transfiguration, by any standards, must be a spectacular event to observe!

Yet all four Gospels do not deal with the Transfiguration of Jesus!

Again, it is John who remains silent.

First, Mark tells us:

"Six days later, Jesus took with him Peter, James and John, and led them up a high mountain, where they were alone. As they looked

on, a change came over Jesus, and his clothes became shining white - whiter than anyone in the world could wash them. Then the three disciples saw Elijah and Moses talking with Jesus..........then a cloud appeared and covered them with its shadow and a voice came from the cloud, 'This is my own dear Son - listen to him!' They took a quick look round but did not see anyone else; only Jesus was with them." (Mark 9:2-8)

And what does Matthew tell us?

Matthew, as usual, copies Mark almost word for word!

Except he has, as well as Jesus' clothes "*dazzling white",* Jesus' face was "*shining like the sun*". And, when the disciples heard the voice, they were "*so terrified that they threw themselves face downwards on the ground". (Matthew 17:1-8)*

Luke then gives us roughly the same version again, except he gets a bit confused! He adds in the bit about how Moses and Elijah "*appeared in heavenly glory and talked with Jesus about the way in which he would soon fulfil God's purpose by dying in Jerusalem".*

Then he spoils it all by saying: "*Peter and his companions were sound asleep, but they woke up and saw Jesus' glory......."* (Luke 9:28-35)

So did the disciples miss the show? Or did they fall asleep in the middle of it?

All rather vague, really!

The Triumphant Entry Into Jerusalem

Let us start with the appropriate prophecy!

Why do we need to start with a prophecy?

Because if we don't have a prophecy, how are we going to have a prophecy fulfilled?

And we know by this stage that fulfilling prophecies is what the Gospels are all about!

Right?

Found one!

"Shout for joy you people of Jerusalem! Look, your king is coming to you! He comes triumphant and victorious, but humble and riding on a donkey-on a colt, the foal of a donkey". (Zechariah 9:9)

"As Jesus and his disciples approached Jerusalem..........Jesus sent two of the disciples on ahead with these instructions: 'Go to the village there ahead of you, and at once you will find a donkey tied up with her colt beside her. Untie them and bring them to me". (Matthew 21:1-2)

And, of course, as usual, Matthew continues with *: "This happened in order to make what the prophet had said come true".* (Matthew 21:4)

Matthew, though, once again, gets the words of the prophecy wrong!

"Look, your king is coming to you! He is humble and rides on a donkey and on a colt, the foal of a donkey". (Matthew 21:5)

So now Matthew has Jesus riding on a donkey AND on a colt?

"As they approached Jerusalem........Jesus sent two of his disciples on ahead with these instructions.......'Go to the village there ahead of you. As soon as you get there, you will find a colt tied up that has never been ridden. Untie it and bring it here". (Mark 11: 1-2)

"They brought the colt to Jesus, threw their cloaks over the animal, and Jesus got on". (Mark 11:7)

"Many people spread their cloaks on the road, while others cut branches in the fields and spread them on the road. The people, whom were in front and those who followed behind began to shout: 'Praise God! God bless him who comes in the name of the Lord! God bless the coming kingdom of King David our father! Praise God!" (Mark 11:8-10)

As Jesus and his disciples approached Jerusalem, *"He sent two disciples ahead with these instructions: 'Go the the village there ahead of you; as you go in, you will find a colt tied up that has never been ridden. Untie it and bring it to me".* (Luke 19:28-30)

"Then they threw their cloaks over the animal and helped Jesus get on". (Luke 19: 35".)

And how did the crowd react to all this?

"As he rode on, people spread their cloaks on the road. When he came near to Jerusalem, at the place where the road went down to

the Mount of Olives, the large crowd of his disciples began to thank God and praise him in loud voices: God bless the king who comes in the name of the Lord! Peace in heaven and glory to God!" (Luke 19:37-38)

"A large crowd of people spread their cloaks on the road while others cut branches from the trees and spread them on the road. The crowds walking in front of Jesus and those walking behind began to shout: 'Praise to David's Son! God bless him who comes in the name of ttythe Lord! Praise God!'...........When Jesus entered Jerusalem, the whole city was thrown into an uproar". (Matthew: 21:8-11)

"The next day the large crowd that had come to the Passover Festival heard that Jesus was coming to Jerusalem So they took branches of palm trees and went out to meet him shouting: 'Praise God! God bless him who comes in the name of the Lord! God bless the King of Israel!'.....Jesus found a donkey and rode on it, just as the scripture says: Do not be afraid, city of Zion! Here comes your king, riding on a donkey.' His disciples did not understand this at the time, but when Jesus had been raised to glory, they remembered that they had done this for him.......The Pharisees then said to one another, 'You see, we are not succeeding at all! Look, the whole world is following him!" (John: 12:12-19)

Yet this same crowd just shortly afterwards were shouting and demanding Jesus' death!

The dots just do not join up!

The figures just do not tally!

The jig-saw pieces just do not fit!

The Last Supper and the Eucharist

The story of the Last Supper is carried by Mark, Matthew and Luke, but not by John. Jesus is portrayed as performing a ceremony, but not, as the Catholic Church has always maintained, as instituting any particular rite to be passed down to future generations.

This was the Jewish Passover meal, of paramount importance to the Jewish people. Jesus, being a Jew, would of course wish to celebrate the Passover meal with his disciples.

The Church refers to this Passover meal as the Last Supper and teaches that it was at this Passover meal that Jesus established the Sacrament of the Eucharist.

The Sacrament of the Eucharist is one of the fundamental teachings of the Church.

So what do the Gospels say about the Last Supper?

Remember! Mark's Gospel was written first:

"While they were eating, Jesus took a piece of bread, gave a prayer of thanks, broke it, and gave it to his disciples. 'Take it,' he said, 'this is my body.'

Then he took a cup, gave thanks to God, and handed it to them; and they all drank from it. Jesus said, 'This is my blood which is poured out for many, my blood which seals God's covenant. I tell you, I will never again drink this wine until the day I drink the new wine in the Kingdom of God.'

Then they sang a hymn and went out to the Mount of Olives." (Mark 14:22-26)

Matthew's Gospel was written after Mark, and we have already established numerous times how Matthew copies Mark almost word for word!

"While they were eating, Jesus took a piece of bread, gave a prayer of thanks, broke it, and gave it to his disciples. 'Take and eat it,' he said, 'this is my body.'

Then he took a cup, gave thanks to God, and gave it to them. 'Drink it, all of you,' he said, 'this is my blood which seals God's covenant, my blood poured out for many for the forgiveness of sins. I tell you, I will never again drink this wine until the day I drink the new wine with you in my Father's Kingdom.'

Then they sang a hymn and went out to the Mount of Olives." (Matthew 26:26-30)

Nothing new here then!

Luke's account was written next:

"When the hour came, Jesus took his place at the table with the apostles. He said to them, 'I have wanted so much to eat this Passover meal with you before I suffer! For I tell you, I will never eat it until it is given its full meaning in the Kingdom of God.'

Then Jesus took a cup, gave thanks to God, and said, 'Take this and share it among yourselves. I tell you that from now on I will not drink this wine until the Kingdom of God comes.'

Then he took a piece of bread, gave thanks to God, broke it, and gave it to them, saying, 'This is my body, which is given for you. Do this in memory of me.'

In the same way, he gave them the cup after the supper, saying, 'This cup is God's new covenant sealed with my blood, which is poured out for you.' " (Luke 22:14-20)

Apart from some confusion here in Luke, where Jesus drinks the wine first, then breaks the bread, and then drinks the wine again, the story is basically the same as that of Mark and Matthew.

There is nothing in any of these Gospel accounts to suggest that Jesus was doing anything more than having a Passover meal, breaking bread with his disciples!

Although John does not tell us much about the Last Supper relating to us instead about Jesus washing the disciples' feet, he does, however, give an account of what the Church calls the Eucharist, in a totally different setting. John's account has Jesus preaching in the synagogue, not at the Passover meal:

" 'I am telling you the truth; he who believes has eternal life. I am the bread of life. Your ancestors ate manna in the desert, but they died. But the bread that comes down from heaven is of such a kind that whoever eats it will not die. I am the living bread that came down from heaven. If anyone eats this bread, he will live forever. The bread that I will give him is my flesh, which I give so that the world may live'.

This started an angry argument among them. 'How can this man give us his flesh to eat?' they asked.

Jesus said to them, ' If you do not eat the flesh of the Son of Man and drink his blood, you will not have life in yourselves. Those who eat my flesh and drink my blood have eternal life, and I will raise them to life on the last day. For my flesh is is the real food; my blood is the real drink. Those who eat my flesh and drink my blood live in me, and I live in them. The living Father sent me, and because of him, I live also. In the same way, whoever eats me will live because of me. This, then, is the bread that came down from heaven; it is not like the bread that your ancestors ate. They later died, but those who eat this bread will live forever.'

Jesus said this as he taught in the synagogue in Capernaum." (John 6:47-59)

However, we have already read all about this before!

And where did we read about all this?

Remember?

We read about it in Paul's first letter to the Corinthians!

"For I received from the Lord the teachings that I passed on to you: that the Lord Jesus, on the night he was betrayed, took a piece of bread, gave thanks to God, broke it, and said, 'This is my body, which is for you. Do this in memory of me.' In the same way, after the supper, he took the cup and said, 'This cup is God's new covenant, sealed with my blood. Whenever you drink it, do so in memory of me.'

This means that every time you eat this bread and drink from this cup you proclaim the Lord's death until he comes.' " (1 Corinthians

11:23-26)

Remember reading this?

But remember also!

Paul never knew or met Jesus!

Paul claimed to have got all his knowledge from visions and visitations to him personally, and to him only, of the risen Christ!

And here is the most important point!

Paul says himself that he got this knowledge, from one of these visions: *"I received from the Lord....."*

It was not from Jesus when he was alive that Paul got this knowledge, because Jesus was dead over thirty years before Paul came on the scene!

Paul is saying that he knows about Jesus' words at the Last Supper by direct revelation, not from hearing about it from any of the disciples who were actually at the Last Supper.

But Paul's writings come before any of the Gospel writings!

So Paul could not possibly have got the story of the Eucharist from any of them!

Clearly, the writers of the Gospel copied from, and were heavily influenced by Paul!

The very thing the Church wanted to cover up!

The very reason why the Church has deliberately placed Paul's writings ***after*** the Gospel writings and ***not before*** the Gospels, where they really belong!

So does this not all point to Paul as being the inventor of the Eucharist?

Could Paul have invented the Eucharist?

Hence, the Gospels copied from Paul, which the Church did not want us to see, so they changed the order!

Furthermore, the followers and disciples of the '*Jerusalem Church*', the followers of '*The Way*', did not observe the Eucharist.

The Eucharist was only observed by those churches which came under the influence of Paul.

And that includes the Roman Catholic Church!

The Roman Catholic Church which adopted the teachings of Paul, not the teachings of Jesus!

On top of all this, we must also remember that Jesus was a Jew!

Such eating of sacrificial flesh and drinking of sacrificial blood was revolting to them by its very nature. It smacked of cannibalism and was certainly not on their agenda!

So, if Paul did invent the Eucharist, from where would he have got this idea?

Remember! Paul was deeply steeped in the Hellenistic Gods and

Goddeses of his time, with all the sacrificial flesh and blood ceremonies that involved!

And of course, Luke was a follower and admirer of Paul!

That explains why Luke's account is similar to Paul's!

Finally, when we think of the actual words the priest says during the Mass at the changing of bread and wine into the body and blood of Christ, whose words is he repeating?

Think!

Is he not repeating the actual words of Paul?

There is nothing more to be said!

Except!

Are those dots now joining up?

Are those figures now beginning to tally?

Are those jig-saw pieces now beginning to fit?

The Betrayal of Jesus

Why did Jesus need to be betrayed?

The authorities could have arrested Jesus any number of times!

Even when the soldiers came for him, and said they were looking for *"Jesus of Nazareth",* Jesus told them "*I am he*". (John 18:5)

Obviously, as usual, to fulfil the prophecy!

Which prophecy this time?

And where can we find one to suit this occasion?

"So they paid me 30 pieces of silver as my wages.

The Lord said to me, 'Put them in the temple treasury'. So I took the 30 pieces of silver - the magnificent sum they thought I was worth - and put them in the temple treasury. Then I broke the second stick, the one called 'Unity', and the unity of Judah and Israel was shattered." (Zechariah 11:12-13)

Matthew obviously, again, creates events in his Gospel to fit in with the prophecies he has managed to find in the Old Testament!

"Then one of the twelve disciples - the one named Judas Iscariot - went to the chief priests and asked, 'What will you give me if I betray Jesus to you?' They counted out 30 silver coins and gave them to him. From then on, Judas was looking for a good chance to hand Jesus over to them." (Matthew 26:14-16)

"When Judas, the traitor, learnt that Jesus had been condemned, he repented and took back the 30 silver coins to the chief priests and the elders. 'I have sinned by betraying an innocent man to death!' he said.

'What do we care about that?' they answered. 'That is your business!'

Judas threw the coins down in the Temple and left; then he went off and hanged himself." (Matthew 27:3-5)

And what did they do with the coins?

"After reaching an agreement about it, they used the money to buy Potter's Field, as a cemetery for foreigners. That is why that field is called 'Field of Blood' to this very day.

Then what the prophet Jeremiah had said came true: 'They took the thirty silver coins, the amount the people of Israel had agreed to pay for him and used the money to buy the potter's field as the Lord had commanded me." (Matthew 27:7-10)

"*With the money that Judas got for his evil act he bought a field where he fell to his death. He burst open and all his bowels spilt out. All the people living in Jerusalem heard about it, and so in their own language, they call that field Akeldama, which means 'Field of Blood'. "* (Acts 1:18-19)

But I thought he gave the money back?

In Matthew, the chief priests buy the field.

In Acts, Judas buys the same field!

In Matthew, Judas hangs himself!

In Acts, his guts spill out!

Matthew says the field got its name because it was bought with '*blood money'!*

Acts says because of Judas' guts spilling and creating a '*bloody*' mess!

"*The Son of Man will die as the scriptures say he will; but how terrible it will be for that man who betrays the Son of Man! It would be better for that man if he had never been born!"* (Mark 14:21)

But Jesus tells the twelve, including Judas they will rule the twelve tribes!

"You can be sure that when the Son of Man sits on his glorious throne in the New Age, then you twelve followers of mine will also sit on thrones, to rule the twelve tribes of Israel." (Matthew 19:28)

And here we have the reason why Jesus chose twelve disciples! To rule the twelve tribes of Israel after his death!

"*So they arrested Jesus and held him tight. But one of those standing there drew his sword and struck at the High Priest's slave, cutting off his ear. Then Jesus spoke up and said, 'Did you have to come with swords and clubs to capture me, as though I were an outlaw? Day after day I was with you teaching in the Temple, and you did not arrest me. But the scriptures must come true.'*

Then all the disciples left him and ran away." (Mark 14:46-49)

"But the scriptures must come true!"

Jesus' own words!

Are the dots joining up?

Are the figures starting to tally?

Are the jig-saw pieces fitting?

The Trial and Death of Jesus

The different accounts of the Trial and Death of Jesus are littered with contradictions.

No surprises there then!

After his betrayal and subsequent arrest, where was Jesus taken?

"Then Jesus was taken away to the High Priest's house, where all the chief priests, the elders, and the teachers of the Law were gathering.......... The chief priests and the whole Council tried to find some evidence against Jesus in order to put him to death, but they could not find any. Many witnesses told lies against Jesus, but their stories did not agree". (Mark 14:53)

All rather vague!

"Those who had arrested Jesus took him to the house of Caiaphas, the High priest, where the teachers of the Law and the elders had gathered together.........The chief priests and the whole Council tried to find some false evidence against Jesus to put him to death, but they could not find any, even though many people came forward and told lies about him." (Matthew 26:57)

Note how Matthew says "*to find some **false evidence** against Jesus"*

Remember, Jesus was framed!

"They arrested Jesus and took him away to the house of the High Priest". (Luke 22:54)

"Then the Roman soldiers with their commanding officer and the Jewish guards arrested Jesus, bound him, and took him first to Annas. He was the father-in -law of Caiaphas, who was High Priest that year. It was Caiaphas who had advised the Jewish authorities that it was better that one man should die for all the people........Then Annas sent him, still bound, to Caiaphas the High Priest." (John 18:12-14; 18:24)

And when did this all happen?

"When day came, the elders, the chief priests, and the teachers of the Law met together, and Jesus was brought before the Council..............The whole group rose up and took Jesus before Pilate". (Luke 22:66; 23:1)

We have just seen how excited and jubilant the crowd were that greeted Jesus on his entry into Jerusalem.

Remember how all four Gospel writers described how the crowd reacted?

Yet this same crowd are now, just shortly afterwards, shouting and demanding Jesus' death!

Why?

What happened in such a short space of time to change things so dramatically?

Matthew, Mark, Luke and John! That's what happened!

They could not portray the Romans in a bad light, so they moved the blame for Jesus' death onto the crowd!

All through the New Testament, the Romans are portrayed in a favourable light, despite the fact that, as we have already seen, they were hated by the Jewish people for the burdens of taxation imposed on them, and despite the fact that Pilate was detested for his brutality.

They even had the crowd shouting that they would take the blame for it all!

"The whole crowd answered, 'Let the responsibility for his death fall on us and our children!' " (Matthew 27: 25)!

The early Christian Church could now point to Jews, and claim they had crucified Jesus!

And despite Pilate's best efforts to save him!

Or so we are told!

The Gospels all have Pilate giving into the mob!

"*When Pilate heard this, he tried to find a way to set Jesus free. But the crowd shouted back, 'If you set him free, that means you are not the Emperor's friend! Anyone who claims to be a king is a rebel against the Emperor!*" (John 19:12)

But it was the Romans, not the mob!

And what else do we know about Pontius Pilate?

We learn about him from three of our historians, Josephus, Philo of Alexandria and Tacitus.

Josephus tells us that Pilate outraged the Jews by several tactless actions, such as using the temple funds to build an aqueduct and introducing military standards and flags bearing the emperor's image, all of which seriously offended Jewish religious traditions.

Pilate's lack of concern for Jewish sensibilities was accompanied, according to Philo, writing in 41 C.E., by corruption and brutality. Philo wrote that Pilate's tenure was associated with "*briberies, insults, robberies, outrages, wanton injustices, constantly repeated executions without trial, and ceaseless and grievous cruelty*".

Pilate certainly would have had no hesitation about executing a Jewish rabble-rouser such as Jesus!

Pilate has been portrayed in all historical writings as meeting all opposition with ruthless force.

Philo of Alexandria describes him as: "*A man of inflexible, stubborn and cruel disposition...... his veniality, his violence, his thefts, his assaults, his abusive behavior, his frequent executions of untried prisoners and his endless savage ferocity......... a spiteful and angry man"*. ('The Embassy to Caligula', p. 299-305)

Pilate himself was a former slave, but became a freedman. However, former slave or not, Tacitus tells us: "*With every sort of cruelty and lust he exercised royal functions in the spirit of a slave"*.

It was Pilate's repeated difficulties with his Jewish subjects that apparently caused his removal from office in 36 C.E., by the Syrian governor, Vitellius, and ordered to Rome to face charges of excessive cruelty.

The Gospel accounts of Pilate's part in the trial of Jesus suggest that Pilate ordered the Crucifixion of Jesus with some reluctance (Mark) or with great reluctance (Luke, John). Many historians attribute these accounts to efforts by early Christians to make their message more palatable to Roman audiences. It is clear that prefects had a variety of options available for dealing with a potential source of trouble, such as Jesus. These included flogging, sending the matter back to the Sanhedrin, or referring the case to Herod Antipas, ruler of Galilee.

Pilate's method of crowd control most definitely did not constitute giving in to them!

"Pilate wanted to please the crowd, so he set Barabbas free for them". (Mark 15:15)

And his method of dealing with someone who called himself '*King of the Jews*' was certainly not lightly! Such past messianic claims had led to civil unrest, and Herod certainly was not about to allow Jesus to go free to create further disturbances and rouse the crowds to feverish pitch!

Yet, this same man, this same Pilate, we are told in the Gospels, yielded to Jewish pressure to have Jesus crucified as a royal pretender, trying to avoid personal responsibility for the death of Jesus!

The dots just do not join up!

The jig-saw pieces just do not fit!

The figures just do not tally!

"*On the way, they met a man named Simon, who was coming into the city from the country, and the soldiers forced him to carry Jesus' cross. They took Jesus to a place called 'Golgotha' which means 'The Place of the Skull'. There they tried to give him wine mixed with a drug called myrrh, but Jesus would not drink it....... It was nine o'clock in the morning when they crucified him........They also crucified two bandits with Jesus, one on his right and the other on his left.*" . (Mark 15: 21-28)

Myrrh is a gum resin used in the making of incense

Matthew tells us: "*They gave him vinegar to drink, mingled with gall*". (Matthew 27:34)

Vinegar is old wine. Gall is a product that comes from the oak tree, used in inks and medicines.

"As they were going out, they met a man from Cyrene named Simon, and the soldiers forced him to carry Jesus' cross...........even the bandits who had been crucified with him insulted him in the same way.: (Matthew 27:32-44)

"The soldiers led Jesus away, and as they were going, they met a man from Cyrene, named Simon who was coming into the city from the country. They seized him, put the cross on him, and made him carry it behind Jesus............two other men, both of them criminals, were also led out to be put to death with Jesus." (Luke 23:26-33)

"So they took charge of Jesus. He went out, carrying his cross, and came to 'The Pace of the Skull'......... there they crucified him.........they also took the robe.......... and said to one another, 'Let's not tear it; let's throw dice to see who will get it'.......This happened in order to make the scripture come true: 'They divided my clothes among themselves and gambled for my robe' ". (John 19:17-24)

And what about the piercing of Jesus' side with a sword?

Only in John is the piercing mentioned.

"They saw that he was already dead, so they did not break his legs. One of the soldiers, however, plunged his spear into Jesus' side..............This was done to make the scripture come true: 'Not one of his bones will be broken'. And there is another scripture that says, 'People will look at him whom they pierced'." (John 19:33-37)

This is obviously taken from Revelation: *"Look he is coming on the clouds. Everyone will see him, including those who pierced him. All peoples on earth will mourn over him. So shall it be!"* (Revelation

1:7)

It's the fulfilling of those prophecies again!

Only each Gospel writer seems to find different prophecies to fulfil!

The Last Words of Jesus

We need to question the last words of Jesus on the cross before he died, as reported in the Gospels!

Jesus believed he was the Jewish Messiah. And he also knew about the prophecies, according to the Gospels!

So he knew he would be crucified, again, according to the Gospels!

So why then, as he was dying, did he ask why God abandoned him?

"At noon the whole country was covered in darkness, which lasted for three hours. At three o'clock, Jesus cried out with a loud shout, 'Eloi, Eloi, lema sabachthani?' which means, 'My god, my God, why did you abandon me?' " (Mark 15:33-34)

"At noon the whole country was covered in darkness, which lasted for three hours. At about three o'clock Jesus cried out with a loud shout, Eli, Eli, lema sabachthani?' which means, 'My God, my God, why did you abandon me?' " (Matthew 27:45-46)

These words echo the prophecy!

Which prophecy this time?

Where can we find a suitable one?

"*My God, my God, why have you abandoned me? I have cried desperately for help, but still it does not come.*" (Songs of David, Psalm 22:1)

Fulfilling the prophecy again!

"*Jesus cried out in a loud voice, 'Father, in your hands I place my spirit!' He said this and died".* (Luke 23:46)

"*Jesus knew by now that everything had been completed; and in order to make the scripture come true, he said, 'I am thirsty'.*

A bowl was there, full of cheap wine; so a sponge was soaked in the wine, put in a stalk of hyssop, and lifted up to his lops. Jesus drank the wine and said: 'It is finished!'

Then he bowed his head and died." (John 19:28-30)

But let us also consider this!

According to the Gospels, Jesus believed he was the Messiah.

Right?

According to the gospels, Jesus also believed that God would appear out of the clouds at any time with his army of angels, to manifest his kingdom on earth. Remember what he said to Peter when Peter cut off the ear of the servant when Jesus was arrested?

" 'Put your sword back in its place', Jesus said to him. 'All who take the sword will die by the sword. Don't you know that I could call on my Father for help, and at once he would send me more than twelve armies of angels? ' " (Matthew 26: 52-54)

Perhaps, indeed, this leads us to a different conclusion!

Could Jesus still have been hoping, to the very last second of his life, that God would yet come and rescue the Jewish people?

This would perhaps make sense of his last desperate words "*My god! My God! Why have you abandoned me?"*

The Burial of Jesus

Only in John is the embalming of Jesus mentioned.

"Pilate told him he could have the body, so Joseph went and took it away. Nicodemus, who at first had gone to see Jesus at night, went with Joseph, taking with him about 30 kilogrammes of spices, a mixture of myrrh and aloes. The two men took Jesus' body and wrapped it in linen with the spices according to the Jewish custom of preparing a body for burial." (John 19:38-40)

Joseph bought a linen sheet, took the body down, wrapped it in the sheet and placed it in a tomb which had been dug out of solid rock." (Mark 15:46)

Matthew says: "*So Joseph took it, wrapped it in a new linen sheet and placed it in his own tomb, which he had just recently dug out of solid rock."* (Matthew 27:59)

"Then he took the body down, wrapped it in a linen sheet, and placed it in a tomb which had been dug out of solid rock and which had never been used." (Luke 23:53)

The embalming of a body in preparation for burial was very important to the Jews.

So why does only John deal with it?

Unearthly happenings

"*It was about twelve o'clock when the sun stopped shining and darkness covered the whole country until three o'clock, and the curtain hanging in the Temple was torn in two".* (Luke 23:44-45)

"*Then the curtain hanging in the Temple was torn in two from top to bottom. The earth shook, the rocks slit apart, the graves broke open, and many of God's people who had died were raised to life. They left the graves, and after Jesus rose from death, they went into the Holy City where many people saw them."* (Matthew 27: 51-53)

That must have been a shock!

I'm afraid Matthew seems to have got rather carried away with the whole thing!

This was reported in Matthew only, written nearly eighty years after the event.

Why did they hang around the graves? I would have thought they would have run for their lives!

And how come such a remarkable occurrence was never mentioned by Josephus or any other of our historians?

Because, of course, it never happened!

It was just yet another story fabricated to have yet another prophecy fulfilled!

The Resurrection of Jesus

Though Jesus is recorded to have said, "*As Jonas was three days and nights in the whale's belly, so shall the Son of Man be three days and nights in the heart of the earth";* (Matthew 12:40)

This, in fact, was not so, as we learn that he was placed in the sepulchre late on Friday and was not to be found there "*early*" on the day after the Jewish Sabbath (Luke 24:22).

That does not add up to three days and three nights! How long was he in the tomb? We don't know.

When he was first seen, Jesus was fully clothed. Where did he get these clothes? His clothes had been divided amongst the Roman soldiers at the cross!

"*After the Sabbath was over, Mary Magdalene, Mary the mother of James and Salome brought spices to go and anoint the body of Jesus.*" (Mark16:1)

But John told us that Joseph of Arimathea and Nicodemus had already anointed the body in the Jewish custom!

Only those closest members of his family would have prepared the body!

Now we hear about Mary the mother of James! But James was the brother of Jesus! So Salome was obviously Jesus' sister!

And was Mary Magdalene Jesus' wife?

There is great confusion, too, over who exactly went to the tomb first and what they saw.

"*After the Sabbath, as Sunday morning was dawning, Mary Magdalene and the other Mary went to look at the tomb. Suddenly there was a violent earthquake; an angel of the Lord came down from heaven, rolled the stone away and sat on it. His appearance was like lightening, and his clothes were white as snow. The guards were so afraid that they trembled and became like dead men.*" (Matthew 28:1-4)

"*Very early on Sunday morning the women went to the tomb, carrying the spices they had prepared.*" (Luke 24:1)

"*Early on Sunday morning, while it was still dark, Mary Magdalene went to the tomb, and saw that the stone had been taken away from the entrance.*" (John 20:1)

And what was the reaction of the apostles to the phenomenal events?

"They and the other women with them told these things to the apostles. But the apostles thought that what the women said was nonsense and they did not believe them." (Luke 24:10-11)

Throughout all four Gospels, Jesus was constantly telling them that he would die and rise again, yet at the end they knew nothing about it?

"They still did not understand the scripture which said that he must rise from death." (John 20:9)

"*They said nothing to anyone, because they were afraid.*" (Mark 16:8)

They "*ran to tell his disciples*". (Matthew 28:8)

"*They and the other women with them told these things to the apostles*". (Luke 24: 9)

"So Mary Magdalene went and told the disciples that she had seen the Lord and related to them what he had told her". (John 20:18)

So many contradictions!

Then we are left with a gap of eight days, when Jesus seems to have just disappeared!

Where was he?

Then, when he does reappear, he obviously needed food, as he asked for some! They gave him some boiled fish to eat.

Now why would a body that was beyond the reach of death, that was shortly to ascend into heaven, need food?

Needing food implies hunger, desire, even digestion!

All of which are of a mortal nature!

So Jesus' body must have been a human one!

He was not a spirit!

And he showed them and allowed them to touch the places of his wounds, on his hands and on his feet, but not on his side!

If the extremities suffered by Jesus on the cross had been fatal, then instantly the work of decomposition would have commenced.

So we must ask, did Jesus really die on the cross?

Did he revive in the sepulchre?

He certainly was not on the cross all that long, and the soldiers did not break his legs the way they did with the others.

That was, so the Gospels tell us, because they saw that he was already dead!

But has Paul not already set the whole story clear for us?

Remember?

"I passed on to you what I received which is of the greatest importance: that Christ died for our sins, as written in the Scriptures; that he was buried and that he was raised to life three days later, as written in the Scriptures; that he appeared to Peter and then to all twelve apostles. Then he appeared to more than 500 of his followers at once, most of whom are still, alive, although some have died. Then he appeared to James, and afterwards to all the apostles.

Last of all he appeared also to me........" (1 Corinthians 15:3-8)

But!

The dots just do not join up!

The figures just do not tally!

The jig-saw pieces just do not fit!

The Ascension of Jesus into Heaven

"*After the Lord Jesus had talked with them, he was taken up to heaven and sat at the right side of God."* (Mark 16:19)

Matthew makes no mention of such an incident!

"*The eleven disciples went to the hill in Galilee where Jesus had told them to go. When they saw him, they worshipped him, even though some of them doubted."* (Matthew 28:16)

"Then he led them out of the city as far as Bethany, where he raised his hands and blessed them. As he was blessing them, he departed from them and was taken up into heaven." (Luke 24:50-51)

John says nothing!

The most important event in Jesus' life and it is dismissed so abruptly!

Very many other unimportant events were reported!

But a central event on which the Christian doctrine is based not even mentioned?

If Jesus had ascended, the news would have spread rapidly!

And of course, we have the usual contradictions!

According to Luke, 24:51, Jesus' ascension took place in Bethany, on the same day as his resurrection.

According to Acts 1:12 Jesus' Ascension took place at Mount of Olives, 40 days after his resurrection. *"Then the apostles went back to Jerusalem from the Mount of Olives, which is about a kilometre away from the city".*

We have nowhere any apostle's own testimony that he saw Jesus ascend into heaven!

John indicates he ascended dressed as usual.

And what does our friend Paul say?

"Flesh and blood cannot inherit the kingdom of heaven".

Does Paul mean by this that a mortal body cannot ascend into heaven?

All rather confusing!

Jesus an Apocalyptic Messiah

As we have already seen, Jesus throughout all the gospels, constantly refers to himself as the '*Son of Man*' and not '*Son of God*'. (John 13:32; 7:62; 7:53; Matthew 10:23; 16:27; Mark 9:9; Luke 21:27)

And three Gospels carry the story under the heading '*Coming of the Son of Man*'.

Jesus himself says he will return in the disciples' lifetime:

"I assure you that you will not finish your work in all the towns of Israel before the Son of Man comes." (Matthew 10:23)

"For the Son of Man is about to come in the glory of his Father with his angels, and then he will reward each one according to his deeds. I assure you that there are some here who will not die until they have seen the Son of Man come as King." (Matthew 16:27-28)

"Remember that all these things will take place before the people now living have all died. Heaven and earth will pass away, but my

words will never pass away." (Luke 21: 32-33)

Mark: "*Tell us when this will be", they said, 'and tell us what will happen to show that the time has come for all these things to take place'.*

Jesus said to them, 'Be on guard, and don't let anyone deceive you. Many men, claiming to speak for me, will come and say, 'I am he!' and they will deceive many people. And don't be troubled when you hear the noise of battles close by and news of battles far away. Such things must happen, but they do not mean that the end has come. Countries will fight each other; kingdoms will attack one another. There will be earthquakes everywhere, and there will be famines. These things are like the first pains of childbirth". (Mark 13:4-8)

Mark : "*In the days after that time of trouble the sun will grow dark, the moon will no longer shine, the stars will fall from heaven, and the powers in space will be driven from their courses. Then the Son of Man will appear, coming in the clouds with great power and glory. He will send the angels out to the four corners of the earth to gather God's chosen people from one end of the world to the other".* (Mark 13:24-27)

Matthew repeats Mark, but adds in: "*The great trumpet will sound*" (Matthew 24:29-31)

Luke then, as usual, embellishes in his own way:

"There will be strange things happening to the sun, the moon, and the stars. On earth, whole countries will be in despair, afraid of the roar of the sea and the raging tides. People will faint from fear as

they wait for what is coming over the whole earth, for the powers in space will be driven from their courses. Then the Son of Man will appear, coming in a cloud with great power and glory." (Luke 20: 25-28)

But! We have already heard all this from Paul!

"What we are teaching you now is the Lord's teaching; we who are alive on the day the Lord comes, will not go ahead of those who have died. There will be the shout of command, the archangel's voice, the sound of God's trumpet, and the Lord himself will come down from heaven. Those who have died believing in Christ will rise to life first; then we who are living at that time will be gathered up along with them in the clouds to meet the Lord in the air. And so we will always be with the Lord". (1 Thessalonians 4:13-17)

Mark: "*When you see these things happening, you will know that the time is near, ready to begin. Remember that all these things will happen before the people now living have all died. Heaven and earth will pass away, but my words will never pass away".* (Mark 13:29-31)

There must be a prophecy we can find to fit in here!

Yes!

Found one!

"*Look he is coming on the clouds. Everyone will see him, including those who pierced him. All peoples on earth will mourn over him. So shall it be!"* (Revelation 1:7)

Now the dots are joining up!

Now the figures tally!

Now the jig-saw pieces fit!

CHAPTER 7:

THE PROPHECIES AND THEIR FULFILMENT

We have already seen in chapter 2 how the Old Testament is full of prophecies, about which the Jewish people would have known.

It is now time to remind ourselves of some of these same prophecies and how they were seen to be fulfilled in the New Testament.

Prophecy: The Messiah would be of the house of David: "*The Lord says: The time is coming when I will choose as king a righteous descendant of David.*" (Jeremiah 23: 5)

This prophecy was fulfilled in the Gospels: "*He (the angel) had a message for a young woman promised in marriage to a man named Joseph, who was a descendant of King David*". (Luke 1: 27)

Prophecy: The Messiah would be born in Bethlehem: "*The Lord says: Bethlehem Ephrathah, you are one of the smallest towns in Judah, but out of you I will bring a ruler for Israel, whose family goes back to ancient times*". (Micah 5:2)

This was fulfilled: "...*and while they were in Bethlehem, the time came for her to have her baby". (Luke 2:6)

However, in the Gospel of John we read:

"But when the Messiah comes, no one will know where he is from. And we all know where this man is from." (John 7:27)

So something of a contradiction here!

Prophecy: The Messiah would be hated for no reason: "*Those who hate me for no reason are more numerous than the hairs of my head; My enemies tell lies against me; they are strong and want to kill me".* (Psalms 69:4)

This was fulfilled: "*If the world hates you, just remember that it hated me first...... they have seen what I did and they hate both me and my father. This, however, was bound to happen so that what is written in their Law may come true: They hated me for no reason at all".* (John 15:18, 15:24)

Prophecy: The Messiah will enter Jerusalem on a donkey: "*Look, your king is coming to you! He comes triumphant and victorious; but humble and riding on a donkey, on a colt, the foal of a donkey".* (Zechariah 9:9)

This was fulfilled: "......*and they took the colt to Jesus. Then they threw their cloaks over the animal and helped Jesus get on. As he rode on, people spread their cloaks on the road*". (Luke 19:35)

Prophecy: The Messiah would be betrayed by a friend: "Even my best *friend, the one I trusted most, the one who shared my food, has turned against me".* (Psalms 41:9)

This was fulfilled, when Jesus responded to the traitor's kiss from Judas, saying to him: "*be quick about it, friend!*" *(*Matthew 26:50) and again: "*When Judas, the traitor, learnt that Jesus had been condemned, he repented and took back the 30 silver coins to the chief priests and the elders. 'I have sinned by betryaing an innocent man to death!' he said".* (Matthew 27: 3-4)

Prophecy: The Messiah would be betrayed for 30 pieces of silver: "*So they paid me 30 pieces of silver as my wages*". (Zechariah 11:12)

This was fulfilled: "*He (Judas) took back the 30 silver coins to the chief priests and the elders". (*Matthew 27:3)

Prophecy: The Messiah would not defend himself: "*He was treated harshly, but endured it humbly; he never said a word. Like a lamb about to be slaughtered, like a sheep about to be sheared, he never said a word". (Isaiah* 53:7)

This was fulfilled: "*But he said nothing in response to the accusations of the chief priests and elders.............but Jesus refused to answer a single word".* (Matthew 27:12; 27:14)

Prophecy: the Messiah will be beaten and spat upon: "*I bared my back to those who beat me. I did not stop them when they insulted me....... and spat in my face".* (Isaiah 50:6)

This was fulfilled: "*Then they spat in his face and beat him".*

(Matthew 26:67)

Prophecy: The Messiah will, say: "*My God, my God, why have you abandoned me?*" (Psalms 22:1)

This was fulfilled: *"Jesus cried out with a loud voice: My God, my God, why do you abandon me?"* (Matthew 27:46)

These are just some examples of the numerous prophecies mentioned in the Old Testament writings and their fulfillment in the canonical Gospels.

And Jesus clearly knew about them!

"*Then Jesus began to teach his disciples. 'The Son of Man must suffer much and be rejected by the elders, the chief priests, and the teachers of the Law. He will be put to death, but three days later he will rise to life'. He made this very clear to them.*" (Mark 8:31-33)

"*Once again Jesus took the disciples aside and spoke of the things that were going to happen to him. 'Listen,' he told them, 'we are going up to Jerusalem where the Son of Man will be handed over to the chief priests and the teachers of the Law. They will condemn him to death, and then hand him over to the Gentiles, who will mock him, spit on him, whip him, and kill him, but three days later, he will rise again.'* " (Mark 10: 33-34)

Then of course as usual, Matthew copies Mark!

"From that time on, Jesus began to say plainly to his disciples, 'I must go to Jerusalem and suffer much from the elders, the chief

priests, and the teachers of the Law. I will be put to death, but three days later I will be raised to life". (Matthew 16:21)

"He also said to them, 'The son of man must suffer much and be rejected by the elders, the chief priests, and the teachers of the Law. He will be put to death, but three days later he will be raised to life.' " (Luke 9:22)

Luke also has Jesus fulfilling the prophecy: *"Then Jesus went to Nazareth, where he had been brought up, and on the Sabbath he went as usual to the synagogue. He stood up to read the Scriptures and was handed the book of the prophet Isaiah. He unrolled the scroll and found the place where it is written: 'The Spirit of the Lord is upon me, because he has chosen me to bring good news to the poor. He has sent me to proclaim liberty to the captives and recovery of sight to the blind; to set free the oppressed and announce that the time has come when the Lord will save his people.'*

Jesus rolled up the scroll, gave it back to the attendant and sat down. All the people had their eyes fixed on him, as he said to them, 'This passage of scripture has come true today, as you hear it being read.' " (Luke 4:16-21)

The trouble with the prophecies, however, is that they contradict each other and a lot lies in the individual interpretation.

It is a bit like reading our daily horoscope! We tend to manipulate things around to make it all fit! Especially if it is favourable!

Exactly what the writers of the Gospels did!

CHAPTER 8:

CONCLUSIONS

"All scripture is inspired by God and is useful for teaching the truth, rebuking error, correcting faults, and giving instruction for right living". (2 Timothy 3: 15-16)

Really?

The bible is generally accepted by millions of people around the world as the Divinely inspired '***Word of God'.***

But with so many contradictions, discrepancies and historical inaccuracies, we need to ask, which parts are divinely inspired and which parts are not? One thing is for sure, they cannot all be!

It would appear that even God can have a few off days!

The divinely inspired word of God?

The words of men, more like! Without the divinely inspired bit!

Having looked at the prophecies of the Old Testament and the writings of the New Testament, and having seen and accepted the contradictions, discrepancies, fabrications and impossible happenings therein, we are now ready to arrive at some conclusions.

- First, we must accept as conclusive, painful though it may be for some, that the Gospels themselves are highly problematic and doubtful as historical sources. We do not have the original texts, nor do we know who were the authors.

- But we definitely know who the authors were *not*!

They most certainly and definitely were *not* the actual disciples of Jesus, those who walked with him on his ministry! They could *not* have been! The dates show that all the gospels were written at least thirty years after Jesus' death.

This means that neither Mark, Matthew, Luke nor John was an actual eye-witness to the events they describe. They heard it all from someone who was maybe there or, most probably, who also heard it from someone else! So the disciples heard about these events then from someone who heard about them from someone else!

- The Gospel stories were handed down orally, for more than forty years, before anyone decided to write them down.

And we all know how that works! Everything is embellished and elaborated to suit a particular purpose.

Chinese whispers!

- Contradictions and discrepancies abound.
- The stories that are common to all of them contradict each other.
- Some events are unique to one Gospel.

For example the escape to Egypt is in Matthew only. But we know why Matthew fabricated it! To fulfil the prophecy! Likewise, Matthew is the only one to carry the stories about Jesus healing two blind men (9:27) and Jesus healing a man who could not speak (9:32). Then Matthew seems to get confused, as he repeats another version of healing the two blind men later on, this time following the version offered by Mark and Luke! (20:29)

Again, as we have seen, simply to have a prophecy or two fulfilled!

- Not all Gospels deal with the major and most important episodes in Jesus' life.

The ascension, for example, is dealt with in only two, that of Mark and Luke. And of course, the virgin birth, which by any standards must have been an event worth writing about, is dealt with in only two, Matthew and Luke.

And even then we saw how virgin births were well established in Greek and Roman mythology and religious cults!

- Not all the Gospels carry the stories of extraordinary events.

For example, Jesus walking on the water, a remarkable event indeed, is carried only by Mark, copied by Matthew and by Luke, but not included in John. The feeding of the great crowd is carried only in Mark and Matthew. Again, an extraordinary event! The transfiguration is carried by Mark, Matthew and Luke, but not by John.

- There is non-historical material.

For example, the Massacre of the Innocents, or the census for the whole Roman Empire.

- They are not independent sources, despite the main Church arguement for them being so.

Yes, they may have been written by different people and at different times, but they all copy from Mark, except for John, who changes the whole story because the end times, as Jesus had prophesised would happen in his own life-time, did not materialise, and so the story had to be changed!

- The authors rewrote history to suit their purpose!
- They were pro-Roman, competing against pagan religions, and so they had to come up with something spectacular!
- They were written in a Roman dominated world.

The Romans were made to look like the good guys. The Jews were shown to be the ones who crucified Jesus, one of their own. Pilate was exonerated. Hence the Romans would have a much greater appeal, being seen as sympathetic to Jesus, while his own people had turned against him!

- The Jews were made the scape-goats!
- Jesus too was framed by the Gospels. The writers wanted to shift the blame for Jesus' crucifixion from the Romans and their cronies the High Priests to the Jews and their religion.

Jesus' main concern was religion not politics.

Jesus' claim to be the Messiah was NOT in any way blasphemous!

The Jews were expecting a Messiah to arrive at any moment!

- The conflicts between Jesus and the Pharisees were fabricated! The Pharisees were the lawyers, the teachers, the repository of Jewish teaching and beliefs. The gospels have Jesus oppose them to depict him as in opposition to Jewish religion! They needed to crucify him on religious charges, propaganda to get the early Christians on the side of the Romans! And the spin was even more embellished by having Pilate defend Jesus!

It was all propaganda! Spin! Fabrication!

And all to have Jesus crucified on religious charges, not political!

The religious charge of trying to do away with the Torah and its teachings!

And we wonder where anti-Semitism began!

And where Hitler got his ideas!

- The Gospels were extensively edited to accommodate the evolving dogma of the Church.
- They were re-edited to substantiate and bolster up certain dogmas of the Church.

For example, the perpetual virginity of Mary or the divinity of Jesus.

- They were written first in Greek. But Jesus and his disciples spoke Aramaic!

- There is often total confusion within the same Gospel.

For example Matthew and the flight into Egypt.

- They differ from the historians of their time!

For example the date of Herod's death and the date of the census of Quirinius.

- Jesus was a Jew, strongly embedded in the teachings of the Torah!

He never came to found a religion! He was a Messiah, who was to free his people from Roman oppression.

- Paul's writings and teachings are the result of his dreams and visions.

Dreams and visions do not exactly count as evidence!

- Why was the order of the writings changed?

Obviously to cover up Paul's alleged post-Jesus writings! And how he would have influenced the Gospels!

- It was Paul through his post Jesus Resurrection visions that made Jesus into a deity, the Son of God.
- Paul would have known about Mithras! Paul was from Tarsus, where the Mithras cult had its origins! Of course he would have known!

But the most obvious conclusions of all?

- The Gospel accounts were obviously influenced by the prophecies in the Old Testament!
- The Old Testament was manipulated to provide prophecies for Jesus to fulfil, as evidenced in the repetitive words of Matthew in particular, to that effect.

Finally, let us look at the respective endings.

First, the ending for Mark:

"*The women went to Peter and his friends and gave them a brief account of all they had been told. After this, Jesus himself sent out through his disciples from the east to the west the sacred and ever-living message of eternal salvation!*" (Mark 16:9-10)

Secondly, the ending for Matthew:

" *Go, then, to all peoples everywhere and make them my disciples; baptize them in the name of the Father, the Son, and the Holy Spirit, and teach them to obey everything I have commanded you. And I will be with you always, to the end of the age.*" (Matthew 28:19-20)

Next the ending for Luke:

"*And as he was blessing them, he departed from them and was taken up into heaven. They worshipped him and went back into Jerusalem, filled with great joy, and spent all their time in the Temple giving thanks to God.*" (Luke 24: 51-53)

And finally, the ending for John:

"Now, there are many other things that Jesus did. If they were all written down one by one, I suppose that the whole world could not hold the books that would be written." (John 21:25)

All neat, compact endings!

Just like a fairy tale! *" And they all lived happily ever after!"*

And when we look on them for what they really are, a series of stories built up around the Old Testament prophecies, a series of stories written to glorify Jesus, to deify Jesus, re-edited to accommodate the newly evolving Christian Church; and when we place them *after the writings of Paul,* and not *before*, as the Church has always failed to do, then we can see the very clear purpose and pattern emerge that the Gospels in the New Testament are very obviously the writings of early Church fathers, building the Church foundation on the writings of Paul. Paul, who deified the human Jesus; Paul who made everything easier from the tougher teachings of the Torah; Paul the Roman, who claimed all his knowledge came from the risen Christ to him and him alone; Paul who invented the Eucharist, as a result of one of his visions! A Eucharist remarkably similar to the blood and flesh sacrificial offerings to appease angry Gods in Greco-Roman mythology and religious cults!

Palestine was awash with hopeful, expectant Messiahs, crying out their words of imminent fulfillment of the prophecies, to any and all who would listen.

Jesus was just another such Messiah.

But what differentiated Jesus from the others, who passed into history, forgotten, left to flounder in the depths of time?

Jesus was rescued from oblivion, saved from receding back into the recesses of time, prevented from fading into the folds of history by being immortalised and mythologised.

And by whom was he rescued?

He was rescued by Paul and the early Church fathers, who saw in his story that which could be manipulated and used to suit their purpose!

The dots now join up!

The figures now tally!

The jig-saw pieces now fit!

And that's the Gospel truth!

If you would like to see what other books Eileen has published, scan the QR code below on your smartphone, or put the URL into your browser:

http://qrs.ly/yq599rm

'A very comprehensive, incisive, logical and well argued debunking of a piece of literature where the results are contrived to match the hypothesis! Post hoc argument!'

P.M.
Psychologist

Made in the USA
Charleston, SC
26 August 2016